Return to Joy

Return to Joy

ANDREW HARVEY
AND
CAROLYN BAKER

RETURN TO JOY

iUniverse books may be ordered through booksellers or by contacting:

iUniverse
1663 Liberty Drive
Bloomington, IN 47403
www.iuniverse.com
1-800-Authors (1-800-288-4677)

ISBN: 978-1-5320-0852-8 (sc)
ISBN: 978-1-5320-0853-5 (e)

Print information available on the last page.

iUniverse rev. date: 10/28/2016

CONTENTS

There is much to get excited about in this book. The authors take up a most important topic--that of Joy along with Justice--that truly characterizes an authentic spiritual path. I am reminded of Thomas Aquinas' teaching that "joy is the human's noblest act" and that "God is supremely joyful and therefore supremely conscious." Yes, the stretching of our consciousness and the reaching of our next stage of evolution as a species depends on a deeper immersion into joy which, as the authors make clear, is distinct from "happiness." An African teacher said to me one day, "what is this think in your Constitution about "pursuit of happiness? One does not pursue happiness. It is already here." This book also assists in understanding the late monk Thomas Merton's question: "How is it possible to tell people they are all walking around shining like the sun?" This book advances the in-depth journey into contemplation and action, mysticism and prophecy, the sacred activism that Earth and her creatures are asking of us all today and it treats the needed shadow with frankness and common sense. A very welcome contribution indeed!

Matthew Fox,
author of *Creation Spirituality* and *A Spirituality Named Compassion*

To begin reading this book is to bring a liberating, luminous clarity to your life. *Return to Joy* delicately, precisely weighs the forces of our modern existence and cracks the heart open with a vision of the deeper reality in which we live. If we are to move forward in our personal lives, in our work on this planet, the message of this book is indispensable.

Philip Shepherd, author of New Self New World: Recovering Our Senses in the 21st Century

A powerful book, rich with wisdom and practical techniques that reawaken and revitalize the boundless joy that lives within each and every one of us!

Linda Bender, DVM, Author of Animal Wisdom, Learning From the Spiritual Lives of Animals

In these times of collective madness and ever-increasing planetary destruction, it is easy and understandable to fall into despair, depression and feelings of powerlessness. As if compensating a one-sidedness in the collective human psyche, Carolyn Baker and Andrew Harvey have done us an invaluable service by writing a beautiful and truly inspiring book on the profound importance of connecting with our joy.

Paul Levy, author of Dispelling Wetiko: Breaking the Curse of Evil

From the first word to the last, Return to Joy draws upon inspiring people and practices, and hard won personal experience, to deliver an impassioned invitation into more authentic, lively living. And true to form, Carolyn Baker and Andrew Harvey bring it all down to earth, making it relevant not only to our personal healing, but also our collective crisis and the hard truths we deny at our peril. This book is a luminous feast—read it not with your head, but with your heart and belly. Feel it! Let it penetrate you! Savor it slowly so that every cell gets a bite!

G. Scott Brown, peacemaker, life coach, and author of *Active Peace: A Mindful Path to a Nonviolent World*

Who could be better to write about embodied joy than Andrew Harvey and Carolyn Baker! These brilliant authors have offered the world a priceless treasure and great inspiration. This revolutionary book is both a transcendent and practical guide to responding to our lives and our world with hope and courage. I feel deep gratitude for their invitation to return to the joy which is our true nature.

Karuna Erickson, co-author with Andrew Harvey of *Heart Yoga,* Director of Heart Yoga Center

Return to Joy explores why embodying joy is serious and sacred work. Andrew Harvey and Carolyn Baker go way past how to cultivate more joy in our lives. They deftly explain why that practice, when coupled with sacred activism, is absolutely vital for our survival on Earth—even when, and perhaps especially when, the world confronts us on a daily basis with so much pain, destruction, and suffering.

Katy Koontz, editor, *Unity Magazine.*

"No return to joy is possible without a frank, searing, and unsparing exploration of everything in our culture that prevents it." These are powerful words that you will read in this gem that will reflect all the riches in you. When we realize that we are all a part of the collective, that we help shape our culture, then and only then are we free to choose Joy. Once again our Mystic Andrew Harvey with author Carolyn Baker show us the way. The joy filled road that leads us to the spirit of love. This book should be on everyone's book self.

Lilly White, Author, Spiritual Coach

In this remarkable treatise, Carolyn Baker and Andrew Harvey bring their wise hearts and minds together—along with the voices of many other revered teachers of our time—to remind us of the truest and deepest sources of joy in life. With climate disruption, species extinction, violence, militarism, and corporate domination all contributing to a global agony, this small book illuminates how joy can guide and sustain us in our daily lives and in our service to the world.

Molly Brown, co-author with Joanna Macy of *Coming Back to Life: The Updated Guide to the Work That Reconnects*

In an era of emphasizing anti-depressants for "fighting" the war against the global epidemic of depression, Harvey and Baker give us a pro-happiness approach to create a world of Joy within and around us. This book is a revelation.

Mona Lisa Schulz

Highly esteemed teacher, author and activist, Andrew Harvey, alongside author, teacher, and visionary Carolyn Baker, whose mission is to "create islands of sanity in a sea of global chaos," have offered us an important new work, Return to Joy. In the midst of the extreme dangers of our time the possibility of accessing joy seems a radical proposal. Joy, however, is born, not of pink clouds of imagining, but is found of at the heart of our deepest sufferings and challenges. We could not ask for better guides on the journey into the our hearts truest nature, a joy that brings forth a wellspring of life-giving hope, energy, love, and capacity. Read this book to open into the secrets of joy.

Thanissara, author of Time To Stand Up,
An Engaged Buddhist Manifesto for Our
Earth.

Messengers of our essential birthright—Divine Joy—Andrew Harvey and Carolyn Baker provide profound and provocative insights into reclaiming our true nature, that of unparalleled joy. This book ignites a renaissance of the soul, presents a radical challenge for rigorous self-assessment, and summons one into the heart's authentic temple of joy.

Karen Rivers, Ph.D. author of Love and
the Evolution of Consciousness

The Return to Joy could only be written by a person who, like Andrew Harvey and Carolyn Baker, have clearly known the centrality of Joy through its source in genuine mystical experience, and through the lifelong task of bringing that experience into space-time life. We are extremely fortunate to have this beautiful and important book.

Lydia Salant and Nathan Schwartz-
Salant, author of The Mystery of Human
Relationship

We've all experienced our share of suffering. To live through the pain of a broken heart seems a rite of passage in this strange and wonderful thing called life. Andrew Harvey and Carolyn Baker's beautiful book found its way to me at a much-needed time—a time when I was in the midst of my own of heartbreak. Reading their words didn't magically fix everything, what they did was help me reconnect to my primordial peace (and considering the state I was in, that's saying a lot). The sacred joy within each of us is our inherent nature, and *Return to Joy* does a wonderful job of guiding us there; for ourselves, for one another, and for the universe as a whole. Please read this special book and experience it for yourself.

Chris Grosso, author of *Indie Spiritualist*
and *Everything Mind*

Return to Joy is the inspiring, loving reminder we all need at this pivotal moment that the ultimate fulfillment of the spiritual journey is joy. As we grieve our beloved planet's descent into the depths of destruction and shadow, we are challenged to remember this timeless truth. *Return to Joy* helps us navigate the way through. Gratitude to Harvey and Baker for their timely, critical reminder of the importance of cultivating joy!

Brad Laughlin
Author/Teacher/Non-profit director

Master storytellers, Andrew Harvey and Carolyn Baker, reveal how love, joy, beauty and grace can be experienced even in the midst of (or perhaps because of) intense suffering, and their gifts to us are to be cherished, read and re-read. Through insight, poetry, and storytelling, the clarity Andrew and Carolyn give us of the ineffable differences between "happiness" and real joy is breathtaking and breath-making. This book is both fascinating and beautiful.

Charlene Marshall,
Wife of the late Ambassador,
Anthony D. Marshall

Books By Andrew Harvey

The Hope: A Guide To Sacred Activism
Radical Passion: Sacred Love and Wisdom In Action
Son of Man: The Mystical Path To Christ
The Essential Mystics
Heart Yoga
The Teachings of Rumi
The Direct Path: Creating a Personal Journey to the Divine
Using the World's Spiritual Traditions
A Journey To Ladakh
Return of The Mother
Light Upon Light
The Way of Passion
Love's Glory: Recreations Of Rumi
Essential Gay Mystics

Books By Carolyn Baker

Reclaiming The Dark Feminine: The Price of Desire
Journey of Forgiveness
US History Uncensored: What Your High School Textbook
Didn't Tell You
Coming Out Of Fundamentalist Christianity: An
Autobiography Affirming Sensuality, Social Justice, and
The Sacred
Sacred Demise: Walking The Spiritual Path Of Industrial
Civilization's Collapse
Navigating The Coming Chaos: A Handbook For Inner
Transition
Collapsing Consciously: Transformative Truths For
Turbulent Times

ACKNOWLEDGEMENTS

We wish to acknowledge all who have supported our work and have enabled us to experience radical joy in our lives and work. Gratitude to Jenny D'Angelo for her superb editing and Caroline Myss, Ellen Gunter, Jill Angelo, Anne Andrews, Matthew Fox, Dorothy Walters, Linda Tucker, Francis Weller, Joanna Macy, and Marianne Williamson for the flame of joy and inspiration they have ignited and tended through the years.

Thank you Andrea Adonis and the editorial, marketing, printing, and distribution staff of iUniverse Publishing.

We extend special gratitude to our more-than-human friends Sammy and Jade and all of the more than human beings on this planet who tirelessly provide life, love, and wisdom to our joy-challenged species.

DEDICATION

This book is dedicated to all of the more than human species of our planet.

Foreword For Return To Joy

By
Andrew Harvey and Carolyn Baker

Mythologist Joseph Campbell often returned to a phrase in his teachings that came out of his studies of Buddhism. He said that the principle aim in life is to "participate joyfully in the sorrows of the world." For many of us, we are all too familiar with the sorrow, but rarely do we know how to cultivate joy. This makes our suffering something we attempt to avoid, overcome, or to rise above. There is something in Campbell's phrase, however, that suggests that joy and sorrow are entangled, forming something akin to a prayer. At this grave time, we are in need of an education of the heart that can once again show us the ways that we may return to joy and be able to hold our suffering, and the suffering of the world, with compassion and generosity.

I have spent many years working with grief. In my writings and workshops, I have seen the wide range of sorrows that we carry in our hearts. Far too often, we are asked to walk with these losses in isolation. When we come together, however, in the company of one another and share these stories of sorrow, something begins to change. And then, in the container of deep ritual, we set our grief down and we return to joy. I have seen this over and over again in our grief ritual gatherings. It may be that we need a village to participate joyfully in the sorrows of the world.

This is a demanding book. Harvey and Baker reveal the wholesale changes we must make in order to find our way back to joy. We are often enticed to believe that change comes quickly and easily. Just a matter of shifting one's perspective or thinking positively. In truth, real change is hard won. It demands everything of us, and only a thorough devotion will suffice. Carl Jung said that change requires three things: *insight, endurance and action*. Insight offers us a new way of seeing, a revised perspective about who we are or how the world works. To hold onto that insight, however, and allow it to ripen, requires endurance. We must be able to stay with the new way of seeing things or it will vanish like last night's dream. We must keep it in front of us, write about it, dance it, draw it, mull it over with a close friend, meditate on it; whatever we can do to keep our attention focused squarely on the insight. Then, maybe then, the insight will have found a new way to express itself in the world as action. Jung said psychology is involved only in the first stage, that of insight. The second two steps are moral matters. To what will we choose to devote ourselves? What commitments are being asked of us which will enable this insight to deepen into an embodied change?

Return to Joy is a book suffused with moral courage, offering us scores of ways to work with the core insight the book offers which states that "joy is the ultimate nature of reality." The authors declare that "the true task in life is to uncover this primordial joy in oneself and then live from its peace, energy, radiant purpose and embodied passion." From this initial revelation, we are asked to take the second step and practice endurance, keeping this insight in front of us. Baker and Harvey say that we must commit everything to this cause. It is because of their steadfast conviction to the work at hand, that I am convinced of their sincerity. The return to joy, it turns out, is not a light matter: It is weighty and requires our ongoing effort. This effort is more of a shedding, however, a letting go of the cultural conditioning that has diminished the wider arc of our lives. Joy, itself, is always available and within our reach. It is, as the authors remind us, the very ground of our being.

We need this book. We need the wisdom and vision that it offers. Baker and Harvey have crafted a concise guidebook capable of reminding us of our deep time inheritance, which is joy. They offer many practices to help us recall that we are creatures shaped for delight, rapture and intimacy. Our entire makeup is designed to drink in the wonder and beauty of this world. But there are many forces that thwart this exchange such as the fact that we live in a "flatline" culture, the rise of the corporate machine, the degradation of the feminine and others. Baker and Harvey look squarely at these forces that oppress our spirit and imprison our minds that often result in an insidious forgetting of who we are, where we belong, and what is sacred. Fortunately for us, they also offer many remedies to this forgetting, an abundance of homeopathic tinctures to help us heal and mend from our long amnesia. Many of them are familiar and ones we might anticipate: beauty, creativity, the Earth, the sacred, but others will surprise us. We are invited to come to joy through conscious grieving, shadow healing, truth- telling and justice-making. Joy comes through many gateways and it is up to us, you and me, to return to joy.

To free the heart, to once again fall in love outwards, as the poet Robinson Jeffers suggests, is at the core of this book. The authors remind us over and over again, that joy is our natural state. It is the true home of the soul. The mystic poet Rumi echoes that statement when he declared the "soul is here for its own joy." I want that in my life and in the lives of our children, grandchildren, and the wider community; joy that is infectious and that keeps our hearts fed during hard times; joy that enables us to step back from the feeding trough of consumerist society. When joy is present, we are enough, and we have enough. Our incessant emptiness is abated and we can cease the relentless search for more.

We need this book. This is a book that peels back the coverings over our hearts and dares us to touch the world again—to fall in love with moonlight and the blue of the sky, the caress of the wind and the smell of rain. Joy is a gateway to awe, wonder and enchantment, the heart enamored with the beauty of the world. We need this capacity now more than ever. When our hearts are aroused, we find ourselves living in a scintillating world, one riddled with wild and fragrant life. Joy illuminates the shimmering world that is, and we are granted a glimpse of the eternal in the here and now.

We need this book. We need what is found here to help us come home to ourselves, to each other, to the watersheds and the great wheeling galaxies. Joy is our true nature. This is cause for celebration.

Francis Weller, Marriage and Family Therapist,
Author of *The Wild Edge of Sorrow: Rituals of Renewal and the Sacred Work of Grief*
Russian River Watershed,
Santa Rosa, California

INTRODUCTION

Nothing is more important for the future of humanity than a global return to joy. At a moment of profound sadness regarding the state of the world, Andrew Harvey was given in a dream vision a message that changed his life. A golden banner was unfurled in a sunlit sky above, and on that banner were written the words: *Joy is the power.* Immediately he understood, viscerally and cellularly, that the tremendous challenges we all face at this time cannot be met by grief or heartbreak or despair alone. What is needed for all of us is to find the way back to what all spiritual traditions know as the essence of reality—the simple joy of being that is the indispensable foundation for all meaningful living and all truly effective action.

We live in a civilization that has lost the essential truth of reality as it has been known in all the mystical and indigenous traditions. In the second decade of the twenty-first century, civilized humans are madly engaged in what is portrayed to them as a pursuit of happiness, but in most cases, they have little experience of joy as the ultimate nature of reality.

The obvious question that arises from this statement is: What is the difference between happiness and joy? This book is an attempt to discern the difference based on the fundamental assumption, derived from the great spiritual and mystical traditions, that joy is the ultimate nature of reality. Happiness is circumstantial; it is a state that as everyone knows, comes and goes. The joy of which we speak is not conditioned by shifts of fate or the play of emotions.

Knowing this makes clear to everyone that the true task of life is to uncover this primordial joy in oneself and then live from its peace, energy, radiant purpose, and embodied passion. This of course demands a lifetime commitment to working with all the forces in oneself that occlude the sun of this joy and becoming clear about all the forces in the world, and especially within our culture, that do not believe this joy is real and sometimes have a conscious agenda to destroy its manifestation.

Living in sacred joy not only reflects the truth of absolute reality but is the ultimate achievement a human being is capable of and the ultimate sign that someone has awoken to their fundamental divine nature and its responsibilities in the world. When asked what is the true sign of a great teacher or an authentically awakened person, His Holiness the Dalai Lama replied, "He or she radiates joy in whatever circumstances arise." This radiation of joy has nothing to do with our current banal understandings of happiness but has everything to do with a rigorous discipline of seeing through the illusions that govern and distort human behavior—and seeing through even the illusion of death, because what is revealed in awakening is the inner divine self that no defeat or ordeal or even death itself can touch or destroy.

True joy is born from this realization. Reading about this or even thinking deeply about this is just the beginning. What has to be undertaken is the challenging and demanding journey towards knowing this viscerally and beyond any doubt.

If you want to live in the joy that is creating all the universes and is your own true father/mother, then you have to undertake the journey of dying to the illusions that prevent you from living in the constant sun of your real nature.

We see the reality of this awakened condition emanating from the presence of the Dalai Lama, shining in the noble face of Nelson Mandela, vibrant in the witness and grace of Jane Goodall, and radiating in the patience and compassion of hundreds of thousands of nurses, doctors, aid workers, environmental activists—ordinary, extraordinary beings of all kinds who have turned up in often very difficult circumstances to commit themselves to the work of love and justice.

These are examples that anyone can relate to, but it is very important to understand that if joy is the ultimate nature of reality, the journey towards it can be undertaken by anyone, whatever they have done and however dark with despair their lives may have become. For example, Milarepa became the greatest saint of Tibet after being a black magician who caused the death of 150 people. Luis Rodriguez, former gang member and prison inmate, is today an award-winning poet on a spiritual path, an urban peace activist who ran for California governor in 2014.

Andrew has worked with African-American men recently released from prison, gang members and murderers who have decided to transform their lives and serve. Is this not the essence of the story of Jesus, who associated with criminals and prostitutes? No one shows this more clearly than Jesus himself, who scandalized the hypocrites of his day by surrounding himself with those whom society had condemned or rejected.

Horrific experiences need not annihilate your opportunities to live in joy. In fact in some human beings it can be the crucible in which a commitment to live in embodied joy is made final.

If you want to live in the joy that the great teachers and servants of humanity have lived, then four things are required:

- First you must accept at the deepest level possible that ultimate reality is sourced from a boundless joy.
- Secondly, you are called to do the rigorous work of understanding the shadows of your past and the psychological labor of clearing the clouds from your essential sun.
- Thirdly, you cannot avoid what all spiritual traditions call us to: Uncompromising and calmly relentless spiritual work to align yourself in all circumstances as much as possible with the powers of divine light.
- Fourthly, as all spiritual traditions know—the greatest joy is only known by those who have not merely tasted divine truth but have committed themselves to the amazing and dangerous task of embodying and enacting it in the world.

This book is created as a guide to reveal how you can come to incarnate this joy. In the first section, we highlight examples of individuals who radiate joy and who inspire us not only with their joy but also the fact that their lives have included suffering.

In the second section, we will explore in detail the saboteurs of joy—those forces in us and in our current civilization that threaten this crucial experience. These must be faced squarely; otherwise, they will undermine any serious attempt to live in freedom and in the energy of joy.

In the third section, we examine the personal and collective shadows that must be made conscious and integrated so that joy can be fully experienced and transmitted.

In the fourth section, we focus on cultivating joy through awakening and through navigating the dark night of the soul into union.

In the final section we present this essential joy as a sun with myriad, interconnected rays, each one fortifying and helping to birth a comprehensive experience of joy in the core of the human being.

At the end of each chapter we offer specific exercises or practices that can be utilized to enhance, deepen, and embody the presence and power of radical joy in one's life.

As you embrace this book and take it to heart, dear reader, our desire is that you will experience the essence of the poet Rainer Maria Rilke's beautiful declaration of joy:

> Joy is inexpressibly more than happiness.
> Happiness befalls people; happiness is fate,

while people cause joy to bloom inside themselves. Joy is plainly a good season for the heart; joy is the ultimate achievement of which human beings are capable. [1]

Andrew Harvey, Oak Park, Illinois
Carolyn Baker, Boulder, Colorado

CHAPTER 1

Joy: The Ultimate Nature of Reality

Since the dawn of our species, humans have been searching for the ultimate nature of reality. Some have posited that virtue is the nature of reality, others propose reason, physical existence, love, truth, justice, and more. In this book we do not argue for any of these, but choose to begin with the quality of joy as offered in the mystical Hindu account of Bhrigu Varuni from the *Taittiriya Upanishad*.

> Once Bhrigu went to his father, Varuna, and said, "Father, explain to me the mystery of Brahman."
>
> Then his father spoke to him of the food of the earth, of the breath of life, of the one who sees, of the one who hears, of the mind that knows, and of the one who speaks. And he further said to him, "Seek to know him from whom all beings have come, by

whom they all live, and unto whom they all return. He is Brahman."

So Bhrigu went and practiced *tapas*, spiritual prayer. Then he thought that Brahman was the food of the earth: for from the earth all beings have come, by food of the earth they all live, and unto the earth they all return.

After that he went again to his father, Varuna, and said, "Father, explain further to me the mystery of Brahman." To him his father answered, "Seek to know Brahman by *tapas*, by prayer, because Brahman is prayer."

So Bhrigu went and practiced *tapas*, spiritual prayer. Then he thought that Brahman was life: for from life all beings have come, by life they live, and unto life they all return.

After this he went again to his father, Varuna, and said, "Father, explain further to me the mystery of Brahman." To him his father answered, "Seek to know Brahman by *tapas*, by prayer, because Brahman is prayer."

So Bhrigu went and practiced *tapas*, spiritual prayer. Then he thought that Brahman was mind: for from mind all beings have come, by mind they all live, and unto mind they all return.

After this he went again to his father, Varuna, and said, "Father explain further to me the mystery of Brahman." To him his father answered, "Seek to know Brahman by *tapas*, by prayer, because Brahman is prayer."

So Bhrigu went and practiced *tapas*, spiritual prayer. Then he thought that Brahman was reason: for from reason all beings have come, by reason they all live, and unto reason they all return.

So Bhrigu went and practiced tapas, spiritual prayer. And then he saw that Brahman is joy: for *from joy all beings have come, by joy they all live, and unto joy they all return.*

This was the vision of Bhrigu Varuni which came from the Highest; and he who sees this vision lives in the Highest. [2]

In the following pages, we ask the reader to embrace the truth that joy is the ultimate reality, far surpassing other qualities named above. What if: "From joy all beings have come, by joy they all live, and to joy they return. He who sees this vision lives in the Highest"? What our time demands of us is that we make the attempt to live in "the highest" by taking the journey that will help experience the joy from which all beings have come, by which they live, and to which they return.

So what is the joy that the mystical traditions celebrate as ultimate truth?

In his short but profound book, *Ecstasy,* Jungian analyst Robert Johnson writes that, "We can say, as the dictionary does, that it is 'an exultation of the spirit, the beatitude of paradise.' We can say that, unlike the ephemeral state of happiness, it is a lasting value that nourishes and sustains the spirit as well as the body. Joy does not induce a craving for more, because it is enough." [3]

In the cultural of industrial civilization, enormous confusion exists regarding joy and happiness. America is obsessed with happiness, but for some years, author and social critic, Barbara Ehrenreich has been ardently confronting the entire notion of happiness and our entitlement to it. In her 2009 book *Bright Sided: How the Relentless Promotion of Positive Thinking Has Undermined America,* Ehrenreich applies the microscope to our happiness obsession and concludes that the popularizing of positive thinking creates blind spots in our consciousness that lead to personal adversity and even such events as the financial crisis of 2008. [4]

If we examine the etymology of the word *happiness,* we notice that it is related to other words like *happen, haphazard,* and *happenstance.* That is because the root prefix, *hap,* pertains to fortune or chance. Sometimes we are fortunate enough to be happy, and at other times, we are, unfortunately, *un*-happy. Therefore, is the "pursuit of happiness" a worthwhile enterprise? Perhaps as Ehrenreich suggests, it would be wiser to consider "the far more acute and searing possibility of joy."

Therefore, let us consider several famous individuals who radiate joy, but whose lives have often been filled with suffering, conflict, oppression, and rejection.

- His Holiness the Dalai Lama: After the invasion of Tibet by China in 1949–1951, His Holiness lived through the cultural revolution in which horrific atrocities of religious persecution occurred, including the destruction of perhaps 6,000 monasteries, the murder and torture of Tibetan Buddhist monks and nuns, and the separation of hundreds of children from their parents. According to the Office of Tibet in Washington, DC:

  Almost a half a century ago, Chinese troops invaded Tibet, bringing to sudden and violent end Tibet's centuries old isolation beyond the Himalayas. Tibet's unique brand of Buddhism formed the core of Tibetan culture and society, a radical contrast to the materialist anti-religion dogma of the Chinese communists. In the wake of the invasion, the Dalai Lama, Tibet's Spiritual and temporal leader, and nearly 100,000 Tibetans fled into exile in India. In the years after, Tibet's remarkable culture and its inhabitants, have been systematically persecuted. Alexander Solzhenitsyn described China's

rule in Tibet as "more brutal and inhuman
than any other communist regime in the
world." [5]

Today at the age of 81, all who come in contact with
His Holiness are moved by his infectious sense of humor,
his vitality, and his inexplicable joy in the face of what he
has endured emotionally and spiritually. He does not simply
speak of joy; he lives and exudes it.

- Jane Goodall: Primatologist, ethologist, and
  anthropologist, Jane spent 55 years studying the
  social interactions of chimpanzees. While Jane's life
  compared to the life of the Dalai Lama or others
  who have suffered great persecution was less fraught
  with challenges, she encountered them nevertheless.
  From the age of 11 she had begun telling people that
  she wanted to go to Africa and learn more about
  apes, but almost without exception she was told that
  girls just didn't do that sort of thing. However, after
  graduation from university, Jane became a secretary
  to the famous paleoanthropologist, Louis Leakey,
  who supported her desire to study chimpanzees
  because Leakey recognized her potential and also
  believed that women made better observers.

Goodall spent decades in the wild, studying chimpanzees
amid very long days alone in an environment that was replete
with danger. Earning the trust of her primate subjects
required years, and was emotionally exhausting—with
no guarantee that it would ever happen. Jane was highly
criticized by her male colleagues for giving the chimpanzees

names, and when she reported that some chimpanzees used tools, she was dismissed with the accusation that they used tools only because she had taught them to do so.

Few people on Earth are as aware as Jane Goodall of the plight of Earth's animal species. It has broken her heart repeatedly throughout her career and continues to do so. Yet Jane radiates joy.

• Tina Turner: Singer, dancer, actor, and author. Tina Turner, who survived a painful, troubled childhood and marriage to a physically and sexually abusive husband, now lives peacefully in Switzerland at the age of 77. Her autobiography and 1984 film, "What's Love Got to Do with It," recounts her humble origins and monumental career success, as well as her decision to embrace a Buddhist-Christian path. As agonizing as much of her life has been, Tina is an international icon of passion, creativity, beauty, perseverance, tenacity, and of course, joy. The wildly sensual and erotic singer of "Proud Mary," "What's Love Got to Do with It," and "We Don't Need Another Hero," has become softened and humbled not only by heartbreaking adversity, but her deepening spiritual quest. Today, Tina declares that, "We're living in world of stars and dust between heaven and all that surrounds us. We're travelers here, spirits passing through, and the love we give, is all that will endure. Just like a rose

7

after the rain, something beautiful remains.... For every life that fades, something beautiful remains." [6]

- Malala Yousafzai: The young Pakistani activist whose commitment to educating women and girls worldwide made her a target of the Taliban. In 2012, Malala was shot in the head three times in a brutal assassination attempt, but miraculously she survived, and after long and tedious medical treatment, she recovered completely. In 2014 she won the Nobel Peace Prize. Her 2015 documentary, "He Named Me Malala," reveals a young woman wise beyond her years, whose mission has not been deterred by the attempt on her life but rather galvanized as a result of adversity. While the name Malala is a variation of another word in the Pashto language meaning "grief-stricken," Malala is an icon of joy with a wicked sense of humor. In her memoir, *I Am Malala*, she writes, "We human beings don't realize how great God is. He has given us an extraordinary brain and a sensitive loving heart. He has blessed us with two lips to talk and express our feelings, two eyes which see a world of colors and beauty, two feet which walk on the road of life, two hands to work for us, a nose which smells the beauty of fragrance, and two ears to hear the words of love."[7]

- Pope Francis: Formerly Father Jorge Bergoglio. Francis was a behind-the-scenes activist in Argentina when that nation was in the grip of a brutal dictatorship in the 1970s. Devoted to the principles of liberation theology, Francis regularly hid people on church property and gave identity papers to people who were opposing the dictatorship. The son of Italian immigrants who moved to Argentina, Francis is familiar with the fundamental challenges immigrants face worldwide, and he is currently championing the rights of immigrants in Europe and the Americas.

In 2015, Pope Francis gave the world his stunning encyclical, *Laudato Si,* one of the most profound statements of spiritual ecology and Earth stewardship ever written. Challenging world leaders, theologians, corporations, and all members of our species, Francis articulated both the gravity and the joy of "caring for our common home."[8]

Joy was the theme of his homily on World Youth Day, 2013, when he stated, "And here the first word that I wish to say to you: joy! Do not be men and women of sadness: a Christian can never be sad! Never give way to discouragement! Ours is not a joy born of having many possessions, but of having encountered a Person: Jesus, in our midst." [9]

Often attributed to Francis is a quote that is not his but originated with Pope John Paul II, yet seems so characteristic of Francis:

> We need saints without cassocks, without veils—we need saints with jeans and tennis shoes. We need saints that go to the movies, that listen to music, that hang out with their friends (...) We need saints that drink

Coca-Cola, that eat hot dogs, that surf the internet and that listen to their iPods. We need saints that love the Eucharist, that are not afraid or embarrassed to eat a pizza or drink a beer with their friends. We need saints who love the movies, dance, sports, theatre. We need saints that are open, sociable, normal, happy companions. We need saints who are in this world and who know how to enjoy the best in this world without being callous or mundane. We need saints. [10]

- Linda Tucker: Linda's White Lion Protection Trust website states that, "After being rescued by a Tsonga medicine woman from a dangerous encounter with a pride of lions in 1991, Linda Tucker gave up a career in international marketing and fashion to become a conservationist. Since then, she has dedicated her life to the urgent protection of the critically endangered White Lions, regarded as the King of Kings by African elders. Despite their rarity and cultural importance, the White Lions have no protected status and may be trophy hunted in the wild and in captivity. To ensure the survival of this legendary animal, Linda Tucker has raised millions of dollars in a long-term strategy to secure large tracks of protected wilderness territory in the White Lions' ancestral heritage lands." [11]

In her 2015 book, *Saving the White Lions*, Linda shares her agonizing journey from being challenged by an African medicine woman to help the lions to creating a non-profit on their behalf while becoming an activist advocating for their preservation. Linda's grueling, heartbreaking, physically exhausting, and legally daunting efforts on behalf of the lions have brought her enormous joy and profound sense of accomplishment. In an online interview with More To Life Magazine interview, Linda states, "What with most of the world's big cats poised for extinction, it's not often today that conservation delivers good news. But I can honestly say: all the blood, sweat, and tears are worth every moment."[12]

• Seymour Bernstein: In conversation with Andrew in *Play Life More Beautifully,* the 88- year-old pianist who was teaching piano at the age of 15, speaks of the joy of accomplishment and the sense of being "played" by life:

> But I have to tell you that I consider myself blessed because when I sight-read music and confront it for the first time, it's analogous to love at first sight when you meet certain people. You don't know anything about that person, but something triggers that love. There are certain pieces that I instantly fall in love with. As I play them, my vocal chords get activated. It's as though I'm exhaling the music through singing. Somehow the music takes hold of me. I have the feeling that there is a special

body part inside of me. And this body part gets permeated with music and *plays me*. It's telling me what to do. It's analogous to someone whispering secrets in your ear: "Now go softer, now go louder, now move ahead, now take a little time." In short I have the feeling that I'm *being played*. It's one of the most satisfying, beneficial, inspirational, and, at the same time, mysterious experiences that I can think of. It makes me exceedingly joyful. And when I realize what the music is telling me, I can't wait to share it with my pupils. They sense that I'm telling them something sacred that they didn't know. Imbued with this new information, my pupils are elated. The circle is completed. [13]

These individuals who radiate joy have lived through various forms of adversity, some to a larger extent than the others, but all are fully engaged in life and demonstrate the likelihood that joy *is* the ultimate nature of reality. They have not retreated from life, but rather embraced it by staying present with their experience and being willing to be remade by it.

In the words of twenty-first century poet, Mark Nepo, author of *Reduced to Joy*, "Another way to speak of joy is to say that it's the reward for facing our experience. Often, what keeps us from joy is the menacing assumption that life is happening other than where we are. So we are always leaving, running from or running to. What keeps us from joy, then, is often not being where we are and not valuing what is before us."[14] Although neither of us wish to compare ourselves with the heroic figures above, it remains true that the work in which both of us are engaged has been profoundly shaped by ordeal and suffering. Andrew's entire vision of Sacred Activism was inspired not only by mystical revelation, but by his own frightening and disturbing dark night of the soul over the course of many years as a result of parting ways with his guru and the storm of abuse and violence that followed.

Carolyn survived the madness of a fundamentalist Christian upbringing and awakened to the devastating truth of planetary destruction. This was attended by two incidences of breast cancer which she also survived.

For both Andrew and Carolyn, the joy that inspires their work is as Mark Nepo writes, the reward for facing their experiences.

SUGGESTED PRACTICES

If you are not already keeping a journal of your emotional and spiritual journey, we suggest that you do so. Even if you do not make entries in your journal every day, it is important to keep the journal close at hand so that you can do so as you wish.

**As you reflect on this chapter, how do you differentiate the meanings of "happiness" and "joy"? What do those words mean to you? What has been your personal experience of each?

**This chapter has provided a snapshot of the lives of several individuals who radiate joy. All have experienced varying degrees of suffering, yet all model joy as the ultimate nature of reality. Reflect on some other individuals who radiate joy. They may be famous or they may be very ordinary individuals relatively unknown to the world at large. How do they radiate joy? How have they inspired you to savor and radiate joy?

**Perhaps the most powerful spiritual practice is also the simplest: the practice of gratitude. When you awake in the morning, give thanks for the simple blessing of being, and consciously celebrate in your life the blessings that you have—friendship, community, relationship. Do this consciously and slowly, allowing yourself to feel something of the depth of each blessing. Do this again before you go to sleep in the evening. Over time, this will assist you in attuning your mind stream to joy.

CHAPTER 2

The Adversaries of Joy

People say that what we're all seeking is a meaning for life. I don't think that's what we're really seeking. I think that what we're seeking is an experience of being alive, so that our life experiences on the purely physical plane will have resonances with our own innermost being and reality, so that we actually feel the rapture of being alive. [15]

~Joseph Campbell~

No return to joy is possible without a frank, searing, and unsparing exploration of everything in our culture that prevents it.

In his 2015 book, *The Wild Edge of Sorrow: Rituals of Renewal and the Sacred Work of Grief,* Francis Weller refers to Western culture as a "flatline culture," the word flatline synonymous with the reading on the medical heart monitor of a dead or dying patient. Noting the numerous obstacles that individuals in Western culture face as they desire to feel and release their grief, Weller writes, "Many of us face challenges when we approach our grief. The most commonly noted obstacle, perhaps, is that we live in a *flatline* culture, one that avoids depths of feeling. We have compressed the range of our emotional lives to the narrowest band. Consequently, those feelings rumble deep in our souls as grief is congested there, rarely finding a positive expression, such as a grief ritual. Our culture, which wants to keep us busy and distracted twenty-four hours a day, keeps shunting grief to the background. We stand in the brightly lit areas of what is familiar and comfortable, not realizing we have lost something essential to the life of the soul."[16]

Not only do we receive overt and covert messages discouraging us from feeling grief, but other emotions as well. Anger in our culture is certainly not acceptable, even if it is expressed appropriately. In recent years, expressing anger or frustration in public is likely to be met with commands to "calm down" at best or suspicion that the angry individual is a terrorist at worst. Fear is demeaned as indicative of an unstable or even cowardly personality. The proliferation of "No Fear" and "Fearless" bumper stickers and T-shirts in recent years confirms how unacceptable the emotion of fear is in our culture, and yet we seem to be marinated in fear as almost daily mass shootings and frequent terrorist attacks around the world dominate the media. Even happiness is, in fact, suspect in the modern world. On the one hand, the masses are seeking it, but at the same time, we are subtly instructed to keep our happiness in check. Only so much giddiness, exuberance, humor, and laughter are tolerated. A psychological diagnosis of "manic" or "bipolar" looms to remind us that too much happiness may be perceived as pathological by the high priests of the mental health profession.

Yet according to Weller, the very suppression of emotion with which we have been socialized is deleterious to our emotional well-being:

> The collective denial of our underlying emotional life has contributed to an array of troubles and symptoms. What is often diagnosed as depression is actually low-grade chronic grief locked into the psyche, complete with the ancillary ingredients of shame and despair…This refusal to enter the depths has shrunk the visible horizon for many of us, dimmed our participation in the joys and sorrows of the world. We suffer from what I call *premature death*—we turn away from life and are ambivalent toward the world, neither in it nor out of it, lacking a commitment to fully say yes to life. [17]

Neither joy nor any other emotion can flourish in the context of numbness. In fact, assuming the role of the well-behaved "flatliner" on the one hand makes us acceptable to a numb and numbing culture, but at the same time, it addicts us to a crazed pursuit of happiness because the anesthetized psyche craves anything that will engender a sense of aliveness.

Moreover, the fundamental underpinning of flatline culture is the socialization of humans as atomized beings, separated from each other, from the cosmos, and from themselves. In his marvelous 2016 book, *New Self, New*

World, Philip Shepherd notes that, in this culture, "The self and the atom are both classically understood to be 'stand-alone' units that interact with other 'stand-alone' units. That understanding provides the foundation for the story by which we live, and that makes it all the more difficult for us to recognize that it is entirely a cultural fabrication sustained by mutual agreement." [18]

Separation has been the scourge of Western culture, and all spiritual traditions have addressed this delusion throughout human history and into the present moment.

The contemporary Buddhist teacher Thich Nhat Hahn writes that:

> Buddhists believe that the reality of the interconnectedness of human beings, society, and Nature will reveal itself more and more to us as we gradually recover— as we gradually cease to be possessed by anxiety, fear, and the dispersion of the mind. Among the three—human beings, society, and Nature—it is us who begin to effect change. But in order to effect change we must recover ourselves....Since this requires the kind of environment favorable to one's healing, one must seeks the kind of lifestyle that is free from the destruction of one's humanness. Efforts to change the environment and to change oneself are both necessary. But we know how difficult it is to change the environment if

individuals themselves are not in a state of equilibrium. [19]

Philip Shepherd emphasizes the word *perseity* or "the quality or condition of existing independently." [20] It violates what Shepherd calls the universal law that we would do well to heed, namely that "relationship is the only reality." [21] Western culture is so infused with perseity that "It is our essential story and our core definition of reality. It is, we might say, the Big Chameleon." [22]

The fundamental enemy according to ancient spiritual traditions—Buddhist, Hindu, Christian, Islamic, and indigenous—is the notion of a separate (false) self that is diametrically opposed to the ancient wisdom of inter-relationship, or as many today are naming it, *Interbeing*. Our notion of perseity is formed by the trauma inherent in industrial civilization, our conformity to convention, and the myriad forms of addiction that permeate the culture of modernity. In fact, Western culture is the ultimate masterpiece of the journey into separation. It celebrates all of the values that keep us partitioned and honors and rewards them luxuriantly.

But how, specifically, does the Big Chameleon of perseity create myriad enemies of joy, manifesting as institutionalized misery in a perpetual pursuit of happiness?

The Corporate Human

Today we are surrounded by various forms of fundamentalism. Some wrap themselves in the guise of religious traditions, others in the assumptions of science and technology. Yet whatever form any particular fundamentalism takes, it limits our creativity, our sensitivity, and the realization of our deeper humanity.

One of the most ubiquitous and offensive fundamentalisms is "the corporate human," and it has succeeded in enslaving the modern world with market values. Yet "corporate" and "human" are diametrically opposed. Although the words "corporate" or "corporation" have their root in the Latin word *corpus* or body, the "body" of the corporation has become the supreme enemy of life on Earth.

Journalist, activist, and author Chris Hedges clearly articulates the history of this enslavement:

> American culture—or cultures, for we once had distinct regional cultures— was systematically destroyed in the 20th century by corporations. These corporations used mass communication, as well as an understanding of the human subconscious, to turn consumption into an inner compulsion. Old values of thrift, regional identity that had its own iconography, aesthetic expression and history, diverse immigrant traditions, self-sufficiency, a press that was decentralized to provide citizens with a voice in their communities were all destroyed to create mass, corporate culture. New desires and habits were implanted by corporate advertisers to replace the old. Individual frustrations and discontents could be solved, corporate culture assured us, through the wonders of

consumerism and cultural homogenization. American culture, or cultures, was replaced with junk culture and junk politics. And now, standing on the ash heap, we survey the ruins. The very slogans of advertising and mass culture have become the idiom of common expression, robbing us of the language to make sense of the destruction. We confuse the manufactured commodity culture with American culture. [23]

Corporate culture embraces fundamentally sociopathic values which negate the truth of the heart and inter-relatedness in favor of short-term profit. Ruthlessness, trickery, betrayal, and winning constitute the brass ring of the corporate milieu. As Hedges argues, we confuse American culture with corporate culture. Reality television shows, monster truck competitions, and extreme sports titillate the senses but manufacture human beings who function in a flatline world—who consume, distract, compete, and plunder, but feel nothing.

No better example of corporate culture and its sociopathic values exists than the economic and political empire of Charles and David Koch. Investigative journalist, Jane Mayer, staff writer for *The New Yorker* magazine and author of *Dark Money: The Hidden History of the Billionaires Behind the Rise of the Radical Right*, exhaustively researched the Koch Brothers empire over a period of five years. Mayer states that, "the book is not just about the Kochs. And the Kochs, on their own, probably would not be able to have the kind of influence they have. But what they've done is kind of a magic trick. They've attracted around them—they've purposefully built what they call an unprecedented network—it's a pipeline, they talk about it, too—where they've gathered about 400 other extraordinarily wealthy conservatives with them to create a kind of a billionaire caucus almost…. it's an organization that I think people need to understand is not just about elections. They've been playing a long game that started 40 years ago, when Charles Koch really got involved in politics in the beginning. And they wanted to change not just who rules the country, but how the country thinks. They're very antigovernment. They are—and they have pushed this kind of antigovernment line for 40 years through many different channels. And it's kind of a war of ideas as much as anything else."[24]

What is crucial to understand about the Koch empire is not simply that the Kochs are unspeakably wealthy and exert remarkable political influence. In the words of Jane Mayer:

> What you have to understand is the Kochs have built kind of an assembly line to manufacture political change. And it includes think tanks, which produce papers. It includes advocacy groups, that advocate for policies. And it includes giving money to candidates. And you put those three together, and they've pushed against doing anything about climate change on all those three fronts at once. So you get papers that look like they're real scientific opinions doubting that climate change is real, you get advocacy groups saying we

can't afford to do anything about it, and you get candidates who have to sign a pledge that—their largest political group is Americans for Prosperity. They have a pledge that says that if you want to get money from this—from their donors, you have to sign a pledge saying that, if elected, you will do nothing about climate change that requires spending any money on the problem. And 156 members of Congress currently have signed that pledge. So, it sort of is a recipe for how to tie the hands of the country from doing anything on this. [25]

In a *Rolling Stone* interview with Mayer in February, 2016, her interviewer pointed out that the Kochs are not going to live forever and that with their passing, their movement might wane. In response, she noted that they have carved out a kind of self-perpetuating empire that has also been set up to draw youth into it. Clearly, the Koch political and economic dynasty will not go away with the passing of Charles and David. [26]

The Koch Brothers are but one example of the corporate reign of inequality by the one percent and a growing sense of impotence among the ninety-nine in the face of the massive power of the ruling elite. They are indeed only two of many poster children of plutocracy.

Conscience, accountability, and a sense of common wellbeing are absent in corporate culture. A glaring, graphic example of this essentially amoral perspective is the debacle of the poisoning of the water supply of Flint,

Michigan, finally fully disclosed in 2016. Not only are profit and power the bottom lines, but in Flint and in hundreds of communities worldwide, environmental racism rules. Violence, poverty, and pollution are ignored and even foisted upon communities of color by white, corporate culture.

Currently, the entire educational system of the United States is crumbling as corporations wait in the wings for public schools in shambles to beg for privatization as the lone alternative to their institutions being permanently shuttered.

Public elementary and high schools in America have become jungles of crime, poverty, neglect, and ghastly illiteracy as masses of abused and neglected children become "wards" of overworked and underpaid teachers who are incessantly overwhelmed by societal nightmares too gargantuan to be addressed in the classroom. The travesty that now constitutes public education in America is a direct result of an educational system that devalues creativity and individual expression in favor of submission to authority and the tyranny of the bottom line.

Maverick educator, John Taylor Gatto writes in *Dumbing Us Down: The Hidden Curriculum of Compulsory Schooling:*

> Whatever an education is, it should make you a unique individual, not a conformist; it should furnish you with an original spirit with which to tackle the big challenges; it should allow you to find values which will be your roadmap through life; it should make you spiritually rich, a person who

> loves whatever you are doing, wherever you
> are, whomever you are with; it should teach
> you what is important, how to live and how
> to die. [27]

But corporate values are incapable of fostering unique individuals because submission to the machine is the ultimate achievement of the modern public educational system. Students are compelled to submit to corporate values and the tyranny of money and are perpetually enticed with the carrot of earning a college degree, which is the ostensible ticket to middle-class existence. Yet in current time, when most American students enter college, they also enroll in a lifetime of debt peonage, confronting a brutally limited job and wage market that severely curtails their ability to purchase a home, escape student debt, or become prosperous members of the middle class. As a result, increasing numbers of American youth are enrolling in colleges in Europe where tuition is free and more employment opportunities are available. Others are choosing not to attend college at all.

In the United States, one is only as secure as one's health and paycheck. As wages shrink and the affordability of health insurance dwindles, employees are increasingly at risk physically and economically. Occasionally, groups of workers organize to protest low wages and lack of healthcare, but for the most part, individuals in American culture are isolated and atomized. They remain overwhelmingly vulnerable, disunited, and manipulable.

As such, human beings become susceptible to constant stimulation and overstimulation, which debases the capacity of each of the senses to experience reality more deeply. For example, visual sensationalism in films can rob one of the capacity to sit in front of a Monet painting for an hour and appreciate its miraculous delicacy. Noise pollution can deaden one's ability to concentrate on and appreciate a Mozart piano concerto. The instant availability of information presented in sound bytes and Twitter-speak corrodes one's capacity to savor language. Mass produced consumer goods, as opposed to handmade items, do not involve the entire body. Rather, they diminish our sense of joy through touch. Thus, the senses of the corporate human are deadened and our humanity hamstrung.

A Death-Phobic Culture

Industrial civilization is a paradigm of power and control. In its obsession with dominating reality and maintaining the illusion of invincibility, it cultivates a universal rebellion against death. Death is deemed "defeat" and antithetical to, as opposed to part of, life.

The poet Rainer Maria Rilke confronted the topic of death directly in his *Letters on Life:*

> Wonders happen if we can succeed in passing through the harshest danger; but only in a bright and purely granted achievement can we realize the wonder... Take your practiced powers and stretch them out until they span the chasm between two contradictions...For the god wants to know himself in you. [28]

At this moment, our planet is literally withering as global warming and abrupt climate change loom not only in the external world, but in our collective consciousness. It is now virtually impossible to carry on an intelligent conversation about climate change without encountering the word *extinction* because many climate scientists and analysts of our predicament inform us that we may have entered the Sixth Mass Extinction on Earth. Whether our own personal death or the death of species, death is ubiquitously a part of life, and no matter how much we rail against its reality, our knowledge of the inevitable haunts us incessantly, even in the face of the plethora of distractions with which we are bombarded by corporate culture.

Thus in the second decade of the twenty-first century, we are witnessing the proliferation of Death Cafés in myriad communities around the world. While some Death Cafés focus exclusively on logistical preparations for death such as preparing proper documents—advanced directives, wills, and power of attorney arrangements—more often Death Cafés invite participants to speak openly about death and share the emotions that surround its reality. After centuries of denying death in Western culture, humans are being compelled to become more intimately acquainted with their mortality and reject the ridiculous sanitizing of their consciousness from death. As a result, many individuals are discovering what all the great traditions have taught: Facing death directly is the gateway to radical gratitude, radical compassion, and radical love. Or as the poet Wallace Stevens wrote:

> Death is the mother of beauty, mystical,
> Within whose burning bosom we devise
> Our earthly mothers waiting, sleeplessly. [29]

Scientific Fundamentalism

Corporate culture is a direct result of the Industrial Revolution, which issued from the scientific revolution of the Enlightenment—that intellectual about-face that occurred in the seventeenth and eighteenth centuries in the West—following what we now call the Dark Ages, which was committed to eradicating the ignorance and superstition perpetuated by the Roman Catholic Church and folk wisdom. On the one hand, the Enlightenment was a breath of fresh air when compared with such commonplace beliefs that women and black cats caused the Black Death of the fourteenth century and the Church's implacable insistence that the Earth, not the sun, was the center of the universe. On the other hand and equally implacably, the Enlightenment committed itself to one path of knowledge only—reason. In doing so, the Enlightenment paradigm, in part, set in motion the paradigm of industrial civilization which glorified logic and the masculine, disparaged intuition and the feminine, and instituted a way of living based on power, control, separation, and resource exploitation. Ultimately, how different the rule of this paradigm was from the hierarchical, fundamentalist domination of the Church is arguable.

The positive legacies of the Enlightenment are many: Learning to think rigorously and critically, questioning authority, freedom from the impediments of superstition, reveling in the delights of understanding our world and making sense of it. Yet, in the last four hundred years Enlightenment enculturation has become yet another face of fundamentalism as a result of its intractable insistence that reason is the only valid method for coping with the vicissitudes of the human condition. This scientific fundamentalism privileges the rational mind and denies the power of intuition and sacred consciousness, cutting off our access to the transpersonal in the name of reason. In fact, the Enlightenment-laden scientific perspective can be an ambiguous chimera which in the words of Kakuzo Okakura causes us to "boast that we have conquered matter, and forget that it is matter that has enslaved us." [30]

In an article entitled "The Top Ten Reasons Why Science Is Another Religion," a biologist with a Ph.D. in Neurosciences argues that science and religion have some striking similarities and often, are not that different: [31]

- Science requires faith
- Most of science is unfounded
- Science will bend to accommodate modern trends
- Science is based on established dogmas
- Science has its own priesthood
- Science has its own code of ethics
- Science makes up stories to explain our origins
- Science reveres its own saints
- It casts out heretics and persecutes all other religions
- Science thinks humans are special

In a 1930 *New York Times* article, Albert Einstein clarifies the authentic relationship between science and religion in a manner that challenges the prejudices of both:

29

It is therefore easy to see why the churches have always fought science and persecuted its devotees. On the other hand, I maintain that the cosmic religious feeling is the strongest and noblest motive for scientific research. Only those who realize the immense efforts and, above all, the devotion without which pioneer work in theoretical science cannot be achieved are able to grasp the strength of the emotion out of which alone such work, remote as it is from the immediate realities of life, can issue. What a deep conviction of the rationality of the universe and what a yearning to understand, were it but a feeble reflection of the mind revealed in this world, Kepler and Newton must have had to enable them to spend years of solitary labor in disentangling the principles of celestial mechanics! Those whose acquaintance with scientific research is derived chiefly from its practical results easily develop a completely false notion of the mentality of the men who, surrounded by a skeptical world, have shown the way to kindred spirits scattered wide through the world and through the centuries. Only one who has devoted his life to similar ends can have a vivid realization of what has inspired these men and given them the strength to remain true to their purpose in spite of countless failures. It is cosmic religious feeling that gives a man such strength. A contemporary has said, not unjustly, that in this materialistic age of ours the serious scientific workers are the only profoundly religious people. [32]

Einstein was one of the phenomenal geniuses in human history who was able to integrate reason and a profound appreciation of the sacred. We could also easily add him to a panoply of famous individuals such as those mentioned above who experience joy as the ultimate reality.

In his "Religion and Science," article, Einstein argued that a "cosmic religious feeling," or what we might call the sacred, motivated him and many scientists to more fully understand the universe. Along with many of his peers such as David Bohm, Werner Heisenberg, Max Planck, Wolfgang Pauli, and Erwin Schrödinger, Einstein championed the rationality of the universe alongside its radiance of divine intelligence. These great minds through quantum physics revealed "*the dancing universe*; the ceaseless flow of energy going through an infinite variety of patterns."[33]

When we are unable to integrate the sacred and the scientific, we become incapable of experiencing joy and align ourselves with its myriad adversaries, perpetuating the vapid pursuit of happiness.

Degradation of the Feminine Principle

In *New Self, New World,* Philip Shepherd states that:

Our own culture...is oriented by its language and art and institutions and aspirations to attend primarily to the male element of doing. For that reason our culture has been called a patriarchy...What we are, I would argue, is *patrifocal*—focused on the fruits of the male element of doing. That focus is rampant in our culture, and it expresses itself in both men and women...and offers almost no provision for a simple, attentive appreciation of Being.

So entranced is our culture with the male element that we tend to justify ourselves in its terms: we commonly define ourselves by what we do and what we have to show for it, and we obsess daily over all the things we have to do or want to do—to which we end we ceaselessly calculate and scheme and schematize and manage and anticipate. And so what if we are out of touch with our bodies and our breath? So what if we have forgotten how to relate to the world as it is and are almost never fully present in it? Look what we are accomplishing, and at what we still need to get done, and at what we should be doing now. [34]

Throughout *New Self, New World*, Shepherd masterfully details the tragic consequences of our patrifocal culture in terms of its disconnection from embodied reality, the values of the sacred feminine, love, relationship, body, interdependence, ecstasy, indigenous consciousness, and celebration. One notably terrible consequence of this over-emphasis on the masculine, is the demonization of passion, which is the key to experiencing the energies of vibrant joy that live in us.

As Rumi so eloquently reminds us:

> Passion burns down every branch of exhaustion;
>
> Passion's the Supreme Elixir and renews all things;
>
> No one can grow exhausted when passion is born!
>
> Don't sigh heavily, your brow bleak with boredom;
>
> Look for passion, passion, passion, passion
>
> Let passion triumph and rebirth you in yourself. [35]

Without allowing divine passion to triumph, how can we be born into our true selves? A flatline culture honors cynicism, irony, relativism, ambiguity, black humor, and a relentless trivialization of any kind of exalted virtue and value. From that jaded perspective, passion, especially divine passion is seen as irrational, an embarrassing intrusion of the hysterical feminine, and purely personal folly rather than an individual expression of a primordial force.

Robert Johnson in *Ecstasy* clarifies the root of the word *enthusiasm,* which literally means "to be filled with God" (en-theo-ism). Enthusiasm is not the same as egoic inflation, which means to be filled with oneself or literally "to be filled with air"—to have one's ego puffed up or to be arrogant. Johnson reminds us that "We must know the difference between enthusiasm, which is entirely legitimate—a visitation of God—and an inflation, which is always followed by a crash of some kind." [36]

In his book on ecstasy, Johnson champions the archetype of the Greek deity, Dionysus, who on the one hand fell into the dark side of ecstasy through excess, yet found divine ecstasy in the sensuous world, "the world of poets and artists and dreamers, who show us life of the spirit as seen through the senses" which is far from the materialistic world of pleasure, destitute of spirit—the world of twenty-first century "happiness."[37]

Religious Fundamentalism

Religious fundamentalism enforces a beatific vision of God and largely sees this world as transient and illusory; it objectifies it and is obsessed with heaven rather than cherishing the planet. Earth is a place to be endured on the way to absorption in the light—heaven. This disastrously devalues human experience, the presence of the divine in nature, and the invitation to transform our world. Inherent in this fundamentalism is the denial of climate change, the fantasy that in all the religions of the book, the world is going to be saved by messiahs who will redeem everyone from the human condition.

Activist Franciscan priest, Father Richard Rohr, of the Center for Action and Contemplation of Albuquerque, New Mexico, notes that "For many Judeo-Christians, God has created a seemingly 'throw-away world.' The so-called 'stone-age' people, the ancient civilizations, the Persian, Greek, Aztec, Mayan, Inca, and Roman empires, even the poor ones we call barbarians, were merely warm-up acts for us. None of them really mattered to God, neither woman, child, beast, nor man. God was just biding his time, waiting for good Jews, Christians, and Muslims to appear, and most preferably Roman Catholics, conservative Orthodox, or Born-Again Evangelicals."[38]

Largely oblivious to the Earth on which they reside, religious fundamentalists seem much more preoccupied with doctrine and "sin management" as Richard Rohr names it, than their relationship with the Earth community. Of this Rohr asserts:

> Our very suffering now, our condensed presence on this common nest that we have largely fouled, will soon be the ONE thing that we finally share in common...At the level of survival we are fast approaching, our attempts to distinguish ourselves by accidental and historical differences and theological subtleties—while ignoring the clear "bottom line"—are becoming an almost blasphemous waste of time and shocking disrespect for God's one, beautiful, and multitudinous life." [39]

Just as Christian fundamentalism has rejected its Earth-based roots in ancient paganism, Islamic fundamentalism has departed from its mystical roots in the Sufi tradition. The central focus of contemporary Islamic fundamentalism is the *jihad* or holy war, which contrary to the mystical tradition of Islam, is now preoccupied with external wars based on the acquisition of resources, territory, and political power.

In the Sufi tradition, it was the spiritual seeker's responsibility to be aware of the *Nafs* or the unconscious ego and its impulses. Jihad was the internal battle the seeker must wage with the Nafs, subduing and refining the Nafs. In *Day and Night on the Sufi Path,* Charles Upton notes that, "The Greater Jihad, and even the lesser one, is really the battle for Love—and the moment you realize this, the battle is won—because when Love takes the field, it meets no opponent...Love is not the *opposite* of hate and the enemy of it; where Love is, there can be no enemy." [40]

Whether religious fundamentalisms wage war on "sin" or upon "infidels," they remain estranged from Earth, condoning and participating in the carnage of military conquest and the degradation of ecosystems. They are inherent adversaries of joy because they ignore or disavow their terrestrial origins and their embodiment in matter. Earthly existence for fundamentalists is a condition to be endured while waiting for transcendent glorification of the body and senses in the world beyond this one.

A more recent fundamentalism, that of New Age spirituality, appears to be blithely oblivious to or only slightly aware of the global climate crisis. While those who embrace New Age teachings may join environmental movements in which they choose to install solar panels, recycle waste, and buy green products, few have carefully researched the horrors of species extinction and the reality of catastrophic climate change. One of the fundamentalist dogmas of the New Age is that any talk of crisis or extinction or environmental destruction or systemic injustice is both negative and actively contributing to the spread of darkness. What is this dogma but semi-psychotic denial of what must be faced and dealt with? In fact, some New Age groups go as far as to argue in an orgy of magical thinking, that "higher" intelligences from other realms of the universe will manifest on Earth in time to save the planet from ruin and that we need do nothing. This kind of fantasy would be hilarious if it hadn't corrupted an entire spiritual movement's capacity to respond to our contemporary crisis with joy, purpose, and dignity.

Fun-damentalism

Yet another enemy of joy is our socially-enforced fascism of fun. Industrial civilization offers us an endless supply of bread and circuses—a continuous morphine drip of fun that is designed to keep us sufficiently entertained so as not to notice the depth of our inner distress and the extent of the destructiveness that our society is wreaking. Whether provided by the entertainment industry, sports, exotic vacations, compulsive shopping, gambling, pornography, or serial romantic encounters, corporate culture incessantly sells the notion that we are entitled to have as much fun as we like, whenever we like, and that we are defective if we are not in constant pursuit of it. Mirroring the cultural scenario in ancient Rome in the waning days of its empire, we are invited to gorge on an unrelenting routine of bread and circuses which serve to distract, enthrall, hypnotize, and gratify the senses. We are invited to settle for the crumbs of pleasure rather than protesting the painful and formidable injustices foisted upon the Earth community by corporate culture.

Philip Shepard notes that, "The idea that we somehow have an obligation to be happy, should expect happiness, or even have a right to be happy creates an invidious phantasm that people chase numbly through all their years, feeling cheated in the end not to have found it. The soul neither wants nor asks for you to be happy: the soul wants you to live—fully, bodily, open to passion and heartbreak and love and awakened to living vibrations of the One. The pursuit of happiness is a soulless enterprise." [41]

The more enslaved by corporate culture we are, the more susceptible we are to its myriad *fun*-damentalisms. The single mother or father working at a minimum wage job, constrained by a mortgage or credit card debt, possibly struggling to repay student loans or just simply subsisting from month to month has little time or energy for activism. Bits of fun can be grabbed on the run for cheap—enough diversion to sustain one in the daily grind for another few hours or days. Meanwhile, where is the joy? *Fun*-damentalisms may mimic joy, but they do nothing at all to alter the modern human's flatline psycho-spiritual status.

As Rilke wrote in *Letters on Life*, "I basically do not believe that it matters to be happy in the same sense in which people expect to be happy. I can so absolutely understand the kind of arduous happiness that consists in rousing forces through a determined effort, forces that then start to work upon one's self."[42]

In our fun-addicted, joy-illiterate culture, we are willing to submit to the various counterfeits of joy in the hope that somehow they will deliver the genuine article, and as with everything else in our industrially civilized world, we expect to experience joy without cost. Yet many of the men and women we highlighted at the beginning of this book who remain shining role models of joy often experienced great suffering in their lives, which served to cultivate a profound sense of joy.

One individual we did not mention was Victor Frankl, the famous Austrian psychiatrist who survived a Nazi death camp. In his wonderful book, *Man's Search for Meaning*, Frankl wrote that "Happiness cannot be pursued; it must ensue." [43] By this Frankl meant that joy is the result of our willingness to be taught by suffering and then to translate that anguish into compassion and service in the world.

Together, Andrew and Carolyn have written a number of books that emphasize the urgency of Sacred Activism in our world as well as the urgency of personal psycho-spiritual transformation. In this book, we wish to emphasize that alongside our commitment to Sacred Activism and the healing of our personal pain, as Sacred Activists we must embrace and embody radical joy. We also know from our own experiences and that of thousands of other individuals, that our willingness to work with the dark emotions dramatically facilitates our capacity to fully taste the joy that is our human birthright. If Victor Frankl could experience moments of radical joy in the midst of the horrors of Auschwitz, so can we in the face of what may be the extinction of life on Earth.

But in order to fully return to joy, we must courageously confront our own shadow and the collective shadow of joy's enemies in our world. Ours will not be a heroic struggle embedded in a spirit of triumphalism, but rather, a sacred warriorship that perseveres in joy regardless of what the outcome may be. It is only such a sacred warriorship, we believe, from our own innermost experience, that will remain focused on continuing to struggle for compassion and justice—even in the extreme circumstances that now seem increasingly inevitable.

SUGGESTED PRACTICES

**In Western culture, we have all been taught to view ourselves as separate—separate from each other, from the Earth, and from ourselves. Philip Shepherd uses the word *perseity* synonymously with this sense of separation, and he calls it the Big Chameleon. How has the Big Chameleon shown up in your life? How is it still showing up?

**How have you been affected by the various "fundamentalisms" of religion or science? How have those impeded your experience of joy?

**From reading this book so far, how is your understanding and experience of joy changing?

**Where do you experience passion in your life? What brings you joy as it is being defined in this book? Make a list of the experiences or activities that awaken your passion and make a commitment to source yourself from passion's energy and power.

**Commit to doing one activity in the coming week that will bring you joy. You may be drawn to express joy or kindness to another person; this may mean engaging in a creative project that brings you joy; you may want to spend quality time with an animal(s); you may want to attend a concert or visit an art museum; or you may choose to spend an hour or more relaxing in nature, drinking in your surroundings with the senses by savoring the colors, sounds, smells, and textures of the Earth. You may want to plant and tend a garden. Options for experiencing authentic joy are endless.

CHAPTER 3

Personal and Collective Shadows: Confronting the Crisis Directly

Dig within.
Within is the wellspring of the Good; and it is
always ready to bubble up, if you just dig.
~Marcus Aurelius, from *Meditations, The*
Essential Mystics, by Andrew Harvey,~ [44]

How hard it is to even conceive of joy in a world in which countless numbers of species are going extinct, including perhaps our own, and so little is being done to address this horror and the unprecedented shadow that it is casting on our consciousness.

The joy of which we are speaking does not depend on denying the agony of our global predicament. Any form of joy that does not directly confront what is occurring is doomed to fail, and at this moment, if we are going to access the creative energies of joy, we cannot afford such failure, for our very survival is at stake.

While the threat of terrorism as a form of short-term extinction is unarguably real, so is the long-term possibility of the end of most life forms on this planet. Terrorism is the ultimate expression of our loss of values, and tragically, countless examples of terrorism are incessantly erupting in what appear to be ordinary, safe places. The November, 2015 attack on people sitting innocently in Paris cafés drinking coffee is but one example of the horrific randomness of terror. Furthermore, the seeming inability of law enforcement to track or check terror and the way in which it is being manipulated politically, intensify the monstrosity that terror has become.

Paralleling the blatant carnage of terrorism is a disturbing savagery in private and public discourse which is given free license on the Internet and pollutes human relationship. It has become another aspect of terrorism in the form of attacks on people which cannot be answered. Gandhi wrote that, "Civility and humility are expressions of the spirit of non-violence while incivility and insolence indicates the spirit of violence." [45] Yet civility in public discourse in current time is almost wholly absent.

Five Collective and Personal Shadows

Shadow is a concept introduced to the Western world by the brilliant Swiss psychiatrist, Carl Jung. In *Psychology and Alchemy,* Jung wrote that:

> The shadow personifies everything that the subject refuses to acknowledge about himself and yet is always thrusting itself upon him directly or indirectly...The shadow does not

consist of small weaknesses and blemishes,
but of a truly demonic dynamic. [46]

The shadow, he said, is that part of the psyche which contains personal qualities we disown because they do not comport with our self-image or who the ego believes we are. Shadow material is that which we say is "not me." For example, we say, *I am not dishonest or lazy or cruel. Other people may be, but I'm not.* Because the shadow is a repository of that which we disown about ourselves, it remains largely unconscious.

In the same manner that individuals carry a shadow, so do communities and nations, and Jung called this the collective shadow. This shadow contains material that the collective disowns and says is "not us." For example, *America is the "land of opportunity," and everyone in America can be successful if they try hard enough.* Or *there is no discrimination in our land or our community; everyone is equal.* Or *they hate us because of our freedom; not because we have exploited or oppressed them.*

While at first blush the personal or collective shadows may seem relatively harmless, they are not. As noted above by Jung, the shadow has a truly demonic dynamic. As long as shadows remain unconscious, they will be projected onto other individuals or groups. Refusal to look at or own the shadow only causes it to expand and intensify. The good news, however, is that we can commit to doing personal and collective shadow work in order to make the shadow conscious and thereby heal it.

This is not, however, as easy as it may sound, especially in the midst of an unprecedented crisis where vast resources are dedicated to keeping the human psyche trapped in an addiction to counterfeit happiness and the superficial satisfactions of consumerism as a soporific to maintain a false sense of security as the planet implodes. Even though the majority of us seem to buy this denial and to continue to exist in a coma about what is really happening, the truth of our situation is that our unconscious is being besieged at all moments by the shadow of what is erupting. This produces in us depression, deep anxiety, despair, and a host of subtle forms of paralysis. In this context the doorway to authentic joy is closed and can only be opened by courageous confrontation of the shadows that our collective crisis is casting on all of us whether we are yet aware of them or not.

We believe that there are **five collective shadow**s unique to this crisis that urgently need to be made conscious:

1) Disbelief or not being able to accept that something so atrocious as the global crisis could be happening. On a collective scale this mirrors the kind of stunned dissociation one might feel being given a terminal medical diagnosis while still feeling relatively healthy. Such disbelief is not only dangerous in that it prevents any kind of meaningful action, it also often leads to accusations of people speaking frankly about the global crisis as "extreme" or "fear-mongering." Once disbelief has been made conscious, it is our experience that the next shadow, denial, unveils its full power for the simple reason that facing the crisis head-on is too painful and overwhelming.

2) Denial, an example of which might be: "Surely global warming is not so severe that it is leading to the extinction of species," or "The mainstream media couldn't possibly be keeping us in the dark about what's actually happening in the world," or "The United States is not an empire attempting to conquer the world. It is simply defending itself against the enemies of democracy." Once denial begins to recede, it is our experience that we become ravaged by the shadow that denial protects us from, dread.

3) Dread threatens to overwhelm us as we contemplate the consequences of our actions in terms of global warming, nuclear proliferation, and attempting to control the world militarily. How could we not dread the blowback that these realities are certain to inflict upon us? Fundamentally, we dread the heartbreak and suffering that are already ubiquitous and bound to get worse, and we are terrified that they will destroy us and drive us mad. Once we have found the strength and clarity to allow this dread to become conscious, we are threatened by overwhelming despair.

4) Disillusion and despair, often attended by molten rage, can feel profoundly hopeless and disempowering, and indeed, the global crisis is more gargantuan and far more severe than we have allowed ourselves to recognize, and our response to it so far is hopelessly and tragically inadequate. Facing this reality is a truly daunting rite of passage and leads to uncovering in the core of the psyche

a death wish born of terror and disgust at what we
are now living.

5) This death wish is a natural outcome of the previous
four shadows. It is a fundamental desire not to be
alive on planet Earth at this time. Many humans
in our time are living with an unconscious or even
conscious death wish because although they may
not be aware of their disbelief, denial, dread, and
disillusionment, they clearly feel it within themselves
because it pervades collective consciousness and
has become infectious. In fact, a flatline culture
cannot *not* have a death wish. Why would anyone
want to live in it? Perhaps our deepest reason for
doing nothing about the crisis is that unconsciously
we may want to see the world destroyed and with
it, a way of life that we have made so futile and
miserable.

Human beings have never experienced what is now
being demanded of us. We are profoundly ill-equipped
and deliberately infantilized by a culture that has every
investment in maintaining our comatose status. There is no
point in pretending that this is not a dire situation, and yet,
there remains, even in this, a way of living our innate joy
nature. But this cannot be born from anything but the most
complete commitment to shadow work. What shadow work
dissolves, we have discovered, is every illusion that prevents
us from diving into our essential joy nature and living it for
its own sake, beyond agenda or any false hope. Only this
can manifest the joy that is our deepest reality.

As well as the five collective shadows, then, we also must confront the five most important **personal shadows** that feed into and collude with the collective shadows.

1) Narcissism. Preoccupation with ourselves is epidemic and prevents us from genuine concern about what is happening around us. We need to examine its presence and its depths in our psyches. Narcissism keeps the death machine operational, and unless it is eradicated, we cannot possibly rise to meet this crisis of epic proportions with grace.

2) Terror of Taking a Stand. We are all afraid of acknowledging what we really know because the kind of demonization we receive from speaking the truth causes us to shrink from doing so. Who among us wishes to be an Edward Snowden or a Julian Assange who must flee to foreign lands and be separated from loved ones and a familiar homeland? Yet we must confront our fear directly and recognize the extent to which we have consented to remain silent and what that consent continues to enable.

3) The Love of Comfort. We are addicted to a lifestyle that we willingly perpetuate even when it is obvious that the world is being destroyed by it. Thus we are unwilling to alter our living arrangements or venture into service in the world that would require our taking risks or moving beyond our comfort zone.

4) Woundology. Rooted in narcissism, this perspective assumes that we cannot act in the world or do deep shadow work until we have healed all or most of

our childhood traumas. Moreover, our private inventory of wounding prevents us from perceiving the reality that millions of beings around the world are suffering far more than we ever have or ever will. But we will never be able to heal our wounds until we make a commitment to serve the healing of others.

5) The Golden Shadow. That is, the adoration of other activists, healers, or celebrities. We allow these people to take action for us because we are afraid to do it ourselves. The illusion is that if we adore this person whom we admire, we are really doing the work that needs to be done. Rather, this is a projection, albeit a positive one, that needs to be reclaimed because what we adore in others are qualities that are crying out to be developed within ourselves but which our adoration prevents us from truly manifesting.

In addition to these personal and collective shadows, we need to notice other aspects of the shadow such as entitlement. It is impossible to live in an affluent culture of narcissism and hyper-individualism without being unwittingly seduced with a sense of entitlement. Ours is a culture of "exceptionalism" that indoctrinates us with the notion that as residents of the First World, we are special and should not have to endure the hardships and deprivation of the developing world, particularly if we are not persons of color. Americans have been fed a "diet" of exceptionalism from birth. While many Americans, and particularly American politicians, are eager to champion

America's 'exceptional' moral purity and military might, few are willing to name the disgraceful ways in which the United States is exceptional: More people incarcerated than in any other nation; a lingering racial divide spanning nearly four centuries, the nucleus of international capitalism and the military-industrial-security complex. Moreover, let us not forget that the United States is the only nation that has ever attacked another country using nuclear weapons.

"Entitlement," Philip Shepherd writes in *New Self, New World,* "is as close as we are likely to come to naming gratitude's dark counterpart, and it seems to be woven into the very cloth of our culture. Consider the extent to which our thinking…is clouded by the agenda of individual rights: I have a right to that, but she has a right to this, which violates my right to those, and so on…Entitlement doesn't require compassion; it requires policing." [47]

Entitlement seen in this light is in fact, the shadow of gratitude. "To detach from gratitude," says Shepherd, "is to slide into self-absorption. No wonder Meister Eckhart advised that 'If the only prayer you say in your whole life is 'thank you,' that would suffice'." [48]

Other shadows include crazed busy-ness in which we have little time to appreciate anything in our lives or be fully present to people and activities. Addiction—a desperate attempt to immerse ourselves in joy, leading only to momentary pleasure and eventually: spiritual, emotional, and physical death.

In addition, corporate culture demands a kind of institutionalized cheerfulness and an obsessive pursuit of happiness in which suffering or the contemplation of suffering is anathema. Grief phobia and grief illiteracy pervade our flatline existence in which we are forbidden to feel sorrow, anger, fear, despair, and even joy. A bit of Disneyland-defined happiness from time to time is acceptable, but it must not linger because if it does, we might be perceived as manic and diagnosed as having bipolar disorder.

And while our flatline status is sanctioned by the culture at large, New Age spirituality in particular bolsters our passionless, institutionalized cheerfulness with its insistence on incessantly having a positive attitude, subscribing to "law of attraction" lunacy, and shaming ourselves with the notion that "we create our own reality." Just as entitlement is the shadow of gratitude, New Age spirituality, shrewdly packaged, marketed, and managed in corporate fashion, is the destructive shadow of embodied, Earth-centered, soul-imbued reverence for the sacred in all living beings. In a deranged celebration of narcissistic happiness, dissociated New Age buoyancy, disconnected as it is from our deeper humanity, derails our journey toward authentic joy and reinforces, rather than eradicates, our personal and collective shadows, making certain the destruction it claims to be protecting us from.

Joy and Happiness: Discerning the Difference

In summary, joy and happiness are radically distinct experiences. Happiness is the low-hanging fruit relentlessly available at a moment's notice to citizens engulfed by the death machine. However, authentic joy, radical joy, requires a price—the willingness to become conscious and live a life of love in action. Victor Frankl spoke of "tragic optimism." By this he meant not only making the best of whatever situation one might be in, but also turning suffering into a human achievement and accomplishment; deriving from the guilt that might arise, the opportunity to change oneself for the better; and deriving from the transitoriness of life, an incentive to take responsible action.

Similar to the perspective of Carl Jung, Frankl was committed to holding the tension of opposites such as "tragedy" and "optimism." Ultimately, profound suffering not only produces the capacity to hold the opposites, it actually compels us to do so. And if we are able to hold the opposites, our suffering often transforms. Moreover, if we do not become overwhelmed by the suffering, which is no easy task, it is possible to notice within it aspects of beauty, grace, irony, and sometimes even a bit of humor.

Pursuing happiness is an effortless endeavor because it asks nothing of us. After all, it is entirely about what *we* are asking from life. However, cultivating authentic joy requires courage because it asks everything *from us*. Indeed, as Richard Rohr notes in his 2011 book *Falling Upward*, many mystics embraced a kind of tragic optimism as a result of their suffering. One example is John of the Cross, who wrote of "luminous darkness" which "...explains the simultaneous coexistence of deep suffering and intense joy in the saints, which would be impossible for most of us to even imagine." [49]

Rohr speaks of a "bright sadness" among the mystics and others who have allowed suffering to instruct them, and he notes that most individuals have a greater capacity to hold these opposites in the second half of life. While this is typical for most inhabitants of Western culture, it is certainly possible for some individuals to hold "bright sadness" or "tragic optimism" in the first half of life. A notable example is Malala

Yousafza, acknowledged above, who at the age of 15 was shot in the head by the Taliban in retaliation for her advocacy for the education of young women. Obvious in all interviews of Malala is the wisdom that is beyond her years—and a wicked sense of humor—but also a "bright sadness" that has been cultivated through tragedy alongside an unquenchable thirst to become a national or world leader who can make a difference on behalf of justice for women and for the Earth.

When we understand the profound differences between happiness and joy, the distinction becomes palpable in the presence of individuals who are pursuing happiness and those who possess "tragic optimism." The "happy" individual is usually content with superficial conversation and usually resists the exploration of issues in depth. Often their thoughts move rapidly from one thing to another, and their demeanor resembles a swimmer ticking off laps as opposed to the joyful individual who may resemble a scuba diver combing the depths. Happy people tend to be preoccupied with accumulating possessions, polishing their status, and being accepted. Whereas the joyful person may be content with time alone in silence, the happiness seeker is usually given to distraction and staying busy. These observations are not intended as judgments but rather as snapshots of the distinction in perception and motivation in the pursuit of happiness versus the cultivation of joy.

Carl Jung was even more rigorous in his assessment of the pursuit of happiness, describing it as:

> The most elusive of intangibles! Be that as
> it may, one thing is certain: there are as

many nights as days, and the one is just as long as the other in the year's course. Even a happy life cannot be without a measure of darkness, and the word "happy" would lose its meaning if it were not balanced by sadness. Of course it is understandable that we seek happiness and avoid unlucky and disagreeable chances, despite the fact that reason teaches us that such an attitude is not reasonable because it defeats its own ends—*the more you deliberately seek happiness the more sure you are not to find it.* [Emphasis ours.] [50]

In a happiness addicted culture, it is crucial to notice the stark contrast between hoping for happiness and the conscious cultivation of joy as a result of metabolizing meaning.

Radical joy is *radical* (a word meaning "going to the root") because it ensues from the root of our being. It is hard won, not mindlessly acquired, as a result of a commitment to utilizing adversity as an advisor and being willing to live a far more expansive and passionate life than the one corporate culture offers us. One can never know the ultimate destination of that journey, but one thing is certain: *Joy is a subversive power, and the price of joy is relinquishing a life of pursuing happiness in exchange for a life of holding joy as the ultimate nature of reality in the cup of one's heart.*

SUGGESTED PRACTICES

**Please ponder the Five Collective Shadows mentioned in this chapter: Disbelief, denial, dread, disillusionment, death wish. How have you in the past or in the present been influenced by these shadows? Journal about these five shadows, not only in terms of their influence on you, but how you have been able to move beyond them, even in small ways.

**Ponder the Seven Personal Shadows and journal about how you have been drawn into them? How have you been influenced by them, and how are you currently moving beyond them?

**Sit quietly without interruption in a meditative space and ponder a recent experience of happiness. How did it feel in your body? Then ponder another experience either recent or distant in which you experienced authentic joy. How did that experience feel in your body? Journal or use a form of artistic expression to record the difference you felt in the body between happiness and joy.

**Describe an experience you have had of "luminous darkness" or "bright sadness" of which Richard Rohr speaks. What was it like to hold these very different qualities alongside each other in your body?

CHAPTER 4

The Myriad Flames of Joy

If you are seeking, seek us with joy
For we live in the kingdom of joy.
Do not give your heart to anything else
But to the love of those who are clear joy.
Do not stray into the neighborhood of despair.
For there are hopes: they are real, they exist—
Do not go in the direction of darkness—
I tell you: suns exist [51]
~Rumi~

As we have noted above, joy is a subversive force, and in our current crisis, the most transforming expression of this force is Sacred Activism. The truest and deepest joy comes not only from recognizing one's essential nature as joy, but in expressing that joy in wise, focused, radical action which implements justice, harmony, balance, and compassion. The joy of which we are speaking is not a private, narcissistic joy; it is a joy that reflects the essential nature of reality and also the deepest meaning of human life as revealed by all the great prophets and mystics of humanity—a meaning that can only be discovered in radical, selfless service and the commitment to a life dedicated to living joy in sacred relationship with all beings.

The radiance of Sacred Activism that we see reflected in the faces of individuals such as Gandhi, Desmond Tutu, the Dali Lama, Jane Goodall, Vandana Shiva, and the many men and women noted in Chapter 1, is like the sun radiating infinite flames. These symbolize the kinds of joy that we need in order to sustain ourselves in the struggles of Sacred Activism and that are required for living vibrantly in a flatline culture. They not only fortify us but support us in enticing others to join us in transforming the internal and external landscapes.

In this chapter we are enumerating a host of flames of joy, but joy's expressions are not limited to this list. We invite the reader to metabolize this list and add to it other flames that erupt from the heart and from one's life experience.

The Joy of Loving the Sacred

When we speak of loving the sacred, we do not mean intellectually or philosophically but rather, with one's heart and soul. We all have the opportunity for intimate encounter with the divine through meditation, contemplation, prayer, and devotion. In other words, authentic love of the sacred must be infused with Eros so that our relationship reverberates with the passionate intimacy we hear in the mystics.

Contemporary Sufi teacher and author, Llewellyn Vaughan-Lee describes the erotic mystical connection as "Living One's Oneness":

> The mystical journey may begin with making a relationship with one's inner light, but the mystic is drawn on a deeper journey toward love's greatest secret: *that within the heart we are one with the divine.* The fire of mystical love is a burning which destroys all sense of a separate self, until nothing is left but love Itself. While the spiritual seeker is drawn to the light of this fire, the mystic is the moth consumed by its flames. Rumi, love's greatest mystical poet, summed up his whole life in two lines:
>
> *And the result is not more than these three words: I burnt, and burnt, and burnt.*

The mystical path takes us into the center of the heart where this mystery of love takes place. Initially this love is often experienced as longing, a deep desire for God, the Beloved, Divine Truth, or simply an unexplained ache in the heart. Mystics are lovers who are drawn toward a love in which there is no you or me, but only the oneness of love Itself. And they are prepared to pay the ultimate price to realize this truth: the price of themselves. In the words of the thirteenth-century Christian mystic Hadewych of Antwerp:

> *Those who were two, at first, are made one by the pain of love.*

Gradually we discover that this love and
longing slowly and often painfully destroy
all our outer and inner attachments, all the
images we may have of our self. The Sufis
call this process being taken into the tavern
of ruin, through which we are eventually
made empty of all except divine love, divine
presence. [52]

For the mystics and for anyone who longs for intimacy
with the divine, an emptying is necessary—an emptying of
ego which allows the fullness of Presence to supplant the
designs and endeavors of the ego.

In her extraordinary book, *The Wisdom Jesus*, Cynthia
Bourgeault clearly articulates the emptying process that in
the Christian mystical tradition was called *kenosis,* which
simply means, "to empty oneself." Kenosis or the kenotic
path, Bourgeault explains, is not the path of renunciation,
which is about pushing things away from oneself; rather the
kenotic path is one of surrender and not clinging. We hear
the notion of kenosis in all of the great spiritual traditions as
Rumi pleads with us to "die before you die" and as Buddhism
cherishes the concept of letting go and relinquishing control.
[53] It may be easier to love the sacred when we feel held and
supported by it and when our lives are humming along
in a manner with which we feel comfortable. Much more
challenging is loving the sacred within us and within all of
creation by surrendering to each moment as it is, even when
external conditions feel ominous, painful, threatening,
unfair, or absurd.

The Joy of Loving and Celebrating Earth

Rumi wrote:

> Adore and love Him with your whole being,
> and He will reveal to you that each thing in
> the universe is a vessel full to the brim with
> wisdom and beauty. Each thing he will
> show you is one drop from the boundless
> river of His Infinite Beauty. He will take
> away the veil that hides the splendor of
> each thing that exists, and you will see that
> each thing is a hidden treasure because of
> its divine fullness, and you will know that
> each thing has already exploded stilly and
> silently and made the earth more brilliant
> than any heaven. [54] [55]

The more threatened and ravaged the Earth community is, the more we are called to adore, cherish, nurture, and protect it. Without Earth, the spiritually erotic relationship which Rumi celebrates, we routinely objectify the Earth and take for granted our relationship with all living beings, and we grow numb to the mind-boggling rapidity with which our planet is withering. The contemporary poet Drew Dellinger captures the essence of Earth eroticism in an excerpt from his lovely poem, "Hymn to the Sacred Body of the Universe":

> 16 million tons of rain are falling every
> second on the planet an ocean perpetually
> falling and every drop is your body every

motion, every feather, every thought is your
body [56]

But no consideration of eco-theology would be authentic
without the poet Mary Oliver, who reminds us in
"Messenger," what our real work is:

My work is loving the world. Here the
sunflowers, there the hummingbird—
equal seekers of sweetness. Here the
quickening yeast; there the blue plums.
Here the clam deep in the speckled sand.

Let me keep my mind on what matters,
which is my work, which is mostly standing
still and learning to be astonished. [57]

The Joy of Loving All Beings as They Are

At this moment, ghastly numbers of species are going
extinct daily. According to the United Nations Environment
Programme, "...the Earth is in the midst of a mass extinction
of life. Scientists estimate that 150–200 species of plant,
insect, bird and mammal become extinct every 24 hours.
This is nearly 1,000 times the "natural" or "background"
rate and, say many biologists, is greater than anything the
world has experienced since the vanishing of the dinosaurs
nearly 65 million years ago." [58]

Now that you have read these facts, please read
them again slowly and contemplate the enormity of their
implications. When you do, you will realize that we have
created an Auschwitz for animals on this planet, and we

have done so because of a hideous failure in love. The only way to transform this failure is to dare to open our hearts to the beauty of the beings that surround us—the animal realm that is so open to giving and receiving love. As animal lovers, both Andrew and Carolyn treasure their pets and experience profound revitalization when they return to their homes and reunite with them physically and emotionally. Through the years, as Carolyn has penned her many books, without exception, one of her canine companions has been lying on the floor nearby. When Andrew returns from an extensive journey abroad, he is infused with the uninhibited outpouring of affection from his cats, who restore his soul with their delicious, mischievous feline presence.

"You only have to let the soft animal of your body love what it loves," Mary Oliver reminds us in "Wild Geese."

What is more, humans have forgotten that we ourselves are animals. *In Becoming Animal,* David Abrams writes:

> Owning up to being an animal, a creature of Earth. Tuning our animal senses to the sensible terrain: blending our skin with the rain-rippled surface of rivers, mingling our ears with the thunder and the thrumming of frogs, and our eyes with the molten gray sky. Feeling the polyrhythmic pulse of this place—this huge windswept body of water and stone. This vexed being in whose flesh we're entangled. Becoming Earth. Becoming animal. Becoming, in this manner, fully human. [59]

We believe that intimate relationships with animals serve as doorways to Earth eroticism—that as our hearts become deeply intertwined with other animal beings, we grow more capable of falling madly in love with the Earth and becoming ferociously intolerant of the abuse and neglect of Gaia. For as David Abrams reminds us: "...it is only the lived, felt relationships that we daily maintain with one another, with the other creatures that surround us and the terrain that sustains us, that can teach us the use and misuse of all our abstractions." [60]

The Joy of the Arts

For our hunter-gatherer ancestors, rudimentary survival was not enough. Early on, they began drawing paintings on the walls of caves and inventing primitive instruments of sound that mimicked the cries of the animals that surrounded them. As the human intellect and body evolved, so did creativity and artistic expression.

One of the most disastrous realities of our time is the minimizing of the arts in favor of technology, sports, and materialism. While many of the super-rich surround themselves with massive collections of art, it appears that the heart-opening humanity of the arts has escaped them. Something profound happens to us when we contemplate a painting by Van Gogh or a sculpture by Rodin. How can we not be moved to tears as we drink in the poignant, tender passion of Debussy in "Claire de Lune"? Who is not shaken to the core by the poetry of Rumi, Rilke, Mirabai, or Emily Dickinson? How can one not be riveted by the theatrical genius of Shakespeare or Oscar Wilde?

What we recognize in visual art, music, poetry, theater, and dance is a force beyond our physical senses. That force is the Presence or stillness within the form. We say that something is beautiful because of the form, but what the form actually exudes is the Divine within the form. Art nourishes, revitalizes, and inspires us because in it, we touch and are touched by the sacred. "Beauty," says Eckhart Tolle, "is not in the form. It is in the Presence that shines through the form. Beauty is about sensing the depth in the form and in yourself." [61] Similarly, Michelangelo is reported to have said, "I saw the angel in the marble and carved until I set him free."

Whether we observe the arts or participate in creating them, we are touching the Divine. In fact, the path of the mystic and the artist and those who delight in the arts is similar. Joseph Campbell recognized this when he said that, "The way of the mystic and the way of the artist are related, except that the mystic doesn't have a craft." [62] [Joseph Campbell, *The Inner Reaches of Outer Space: Metaphor as Myth and as Religion*, New World Library, 2002, p. 128.]

We must approach art in a manner similar to approaching the Earth—with awe and holy eroticism. We engage all of our senses with both nature and art and discover that we are moved so profoundly we will never be the same.

We need not label ourselves as artists in order to create beauty. We can create beauty in our home by making our space sacred. In her 2015 book *Sacred Space*, Jill Angelo writes, "Everything we do affects everything else. It follows that every conscious decision we make about what belongs where in our homes—whether it's the way the space looks, the sounds we want to surround ourselves with or the textures and smells that ground each room—everything contributes to the special grace that makes the sounds we want to surround our self with or the textures and smells that ground each room—everything contributes to the special grace that makes each of us unique." [63]

We must recognize that anytime we creating anything—a project, a beautiful home, a garden, or an actual work of art, we are expressing ourselves artistically, and Presence is flowing through us. The more consciously open to that flow we are, the more beauty we create in the world, and the more energizing potential that beauty holds. Loving and cherishing art in all of its forms can keep us secretly fueled with the energy of creative joy regardless of what is occurring in our world.

The Joy of Play

As you read the word "play," if you find yourself recoiling with discomfort, it is likely that you need this particular flame of joy more than you can imagine. Readers of this book are likely to be activists or deep thinkers who live in a more cerebral world than those who might not pick up this book. Anglo-Saxons in particular have a great deal of difficulty enjoying play or even knowing what play is.

The remarkable Greek sage Socrates learned to play a musical instrument while he was in prison so that he could participate in the great play of the universe, and this form of play provided him the joy, inspiration, relaxation, spaciousness, and the energy he needed to accept his death and not be beaten down. Likewise, the Dalai Lama, a man filled with abundant joy and humor, often sits with mechanical toys and plays with them, and this sustains him in the grueling, protracted struggle of witnessing the pain of the world and constantly pouring himself out to serve others.

In order to persevere in witnessing the suffering in this age of despair, we must learn how to play and balance our striving with relaxation, humor, and lightheartedness. Indeed, the great wisdom traditions teach that divine bliss, or as we are naming it, *radical joy*, is always in the highest sense playing and waiting to invite us also into its all-transforming game of love.

The Joy of Sacred Relationship

As Carolyn has emphasized with resounding clarity in her 2015 book *Love in the Age of Ecological Apocalypse: Cultivating the Relationships We Need to Thrive,* when the world is passing through an enormous death, when people are suffering horribly, when the structures we have lived by are falling apart, the most important thing any of us can do at the core of our lives is to love our friends passionately. If we are fortunate enough to connect with a lover or life partner with whom we can share erotic love and sexual passion, we must love them with all our hearts. In these turbulent times of upheaval and despair, great skill, patience, and compassion are required to maintain life partnerships as well as relationships with family and friends.

This requires of us nothing less than the transformation of our dualistic illusions of separation from all of life. To find the joy of sacred relationship that we need so urgently to fuel our service in the world, we must allow ourselves to experience a radical redefinition of kindness in all relationships—a "tantra of tenderness" that embraces all living beings.

In Naomi Shihab Nye's extraordinary poem "Kindness," she tells us that in order to really know kindness, we must experience loss. Echoing what we have emphasized throughout this book, Nye suggests that kindness takes root in us in a manner similar to the way in which we discover joy: through suffering. Thus she concludes:

> Then it is only kindness that makes sense
> anymore, only kindness that ties your shoes
> and sends you out into the day to mail
> letters and purchase bread, only kindness
> that raises its head from the crowd of the
> world to say it is I you have been looking
> for, and then goes with you everywhere like
> a shadow or a friend. [64]

Demonstrating kindness in our numbed, entranced, narcissistic culture is a spiritual practice and one that we must incorporate in every relationship, no matter how brief or superficial. We can attest to the powerful impact of practicing kindness with a store clerk, a bus driver, a food server, or a customer service agent in person or by telephone. In every human relationship, it is our divine mandate to exude kindness and compassion, even in the most challenging situations, until it becomes "like a shadow or a friend." Such tenderness is infectious and incites reverberations of joy within other human beings and within ourselves.

The Joy of Truth-Telling and Justice-Making

Although we have devoted an entire chapter to the Joy of Service and Sacred Activism, there is yet another joy that makes it possible to engage in these and also liberates us from the collective shadow that engulfs our world. As we confront the realities of catastrophic climate change, the disappearance of species, the potential extinction of all life on Earth, the possibility of endless war, ghastly economic inequality, the horrific oppression of human trafficking and sexual exploitation, the worldwide epidemic of countless forms of addiction, the plight of millions of war and climate refugees around the world seeking safety and sanctuary— as deplorable as these realities are, they *are* what is so in the history of our species at this moment. To deny the horror, on the one hand, keeps us comfortable in the short term, but in the longer term, our denial has a debilitating consequence as it becomes an increasingly onerous burden in the unconscious mind and by extension, the body.

In his blogpost, *The Archdruid Report,* in a post entitled "The Burden of Denial," John Michael Greer writes:

> ...the worse things get, the more effort will go into the pretense that nothing is wrong at all, and the majority will cling like grim death to that pretense until it drags them under. That said, a substantial minority might make a different choice: to let go of the burden of denial soon enough to matter, to let themselves plunge through those moments of terror and freedom, and

to haul themselves up, shaken but alive,
onto the unfamiliar shores of the future. [65]

In our work in recent years we have consistently offered support and inspiration to those individuals who are willing to cast off the burden of denial and befriend the dark emotions that invariably attend our willingness to see what is so. Although disorienting, unfamiliar, and daunting, the joy of truth-telling and justice-making—the joy of in some sense, standing outside the culture of the planetary death machine, seeing it for what it is, and endeavoring to be love in action in an age of despair—this is the radical joy radiated in the beaming face of the Dalai Lama, the indefatigable cheerfulness of Desmond Tutu, and the tears of joy running down the face of Martin Luther King, Jr. when he spoke of having been to the mountaintop. This is the joy born of heartbreak—the joy that ripens into exquisite compassion. This compassion, Eckhart Tolle reminds us, "…does not happen until sadness merges with joy, the joy of Being beyond form, the joy of eternal life." [66]

The Joy of Conscious Grieving

Placing the words *joy* and *grieving* in the same sentence may seem absurd. After all, what does one have to do with the other? In fact, we have experienced that joy and grief are inextricably connected as our friend Francis Weller articulates so beautifully in his lovely 2016 book, *The Wild Edge of Sorrow: Rituals of Renewal and the Sacred Work of Grief.* Francis speaks of developing an "apprenticeship with sorrow," meaning that we make a commitment to feel our grief and allow it to become a teacher. Of this he writes:

> Every one of us must undertake an
> *apprenticeship with sorrow*. We must
> learn the art and craft of grief, discover
> the profound ways it ripens and deepens
> us…It takes outrageous courage to face
> outrageous loss. This is precisely what we
> are being called to do. Any loss, whether
> deeply personal or one of those that swirl
> around us in the wider world, calls us to
> full-heartedness, for that is the meaning
> of courage. To honor our grief, to grant it
> space and time in our frantic world, is to
> fulfill a covenant with soul—to welcome
> all that is, thereby granting room for our
> most authentic life. [67]

Francis once visited the Dagara tribe in Burkina Faso in West Africa where he participated in a Dagara grief ritual which occurs at least once a week in the village. The people of the tribe believe that if they do not release their grief often, it become toxic to themselves and to the community. Francis reports that after the ritual, he encountered a Dagara woman walking through the village smiling and beaming with joy. He approached her and inquired if she had attended the grief ritual. She said that she had and then added that the reason she looked so happy was that she cries all the time.

The famous poet William Blake is reported to have said that the deeper the sorrow, the greater the joy. More recently, Mary Oliver wrote that "We shake with joy, we shake with grief. What a time they have, these two, housed as they are in the same body." [68] Having worked with hundreds of individuals over the years, we have noticed that when people allow their grief in a safe and supportive venue, whether that is in a formal grief workshop or ritual, or it is with a group of supportive friends, they feel lighter, more alive, and have much more capacity for experiencing joy. We believe that grief and joy travel together and need each other throughout the duration of our lives.

The Joy of Shadow Healing

Earlier in this book we have spoken of the shadow, and our experience verifies that all of us must become familiar with the shadow in ourselves as well as the collective shadow of our world and our communities; otherwise we project it on others or act it out. Admittedly, healing the shadow is hard work and often painful because we are committing to looking consciously at parts of ourselves that we would rather ignore or project upon other individuals or groups. Yet in Carolyn's 2016 book, *Dark Gold: The Human Shadow and the Global Crisis,* a treasure-trove of practices and exercises are offered for doing conscious shadow healing. Carl Jung spoke and wrote on a host of occasions about the "gold" that lies buried in the shadow. By this he meant that if we are willing to consciously work on shadow healing, we will discover that gold in the form of unknown and untapped creative energy, undiscovered compassion, and the disclosure of gifts that we may be only vaguely aware of.

Mining the dark energies of the shadow takes great courage. In the process we are often compelled to notice aspects of ourselves that evoke sorrow, embarrassment, fear, or a sense of inadequacy and defeat. If we are willing to persevere in exposing the shadow to our consciousness, and if we are committed to sitting with these feelings as we do so, we are likely to discover the gold in the shadow and ultimately facilitate its integration into the psyche. Invariably, this results in a profound sense of joy, humility, and gratitude that the energy we have expended in repressing the shadow is now available to us to live more passionately and creatively than we dreamed possible.

The Joy of Simplicity

All of the great spiritual traditions have emphasized simplicity. In the Christian tradition we are compelled to notice Jesus, who was essentially homeless during the last years of his life. While constantly roaming the Galilean landscape with his disciples, he often slept outdoors and had no possessions beyond the clothing on his back. His sermons and parables were replete with instructions about living simply, generously, and walking lightly on the Earth in terms of possessions.

The Buddhist, Hindu, and Taoist traditions encouraged spiritual, not material abundance. Lao-tzu reportedly said, "He who knows he has enough is rich." And Gandhi wrote that, "Civilization, in the real sense of the term, consists not in the multiplication, but in the deliberate and voluntary reduction of wants. This alone promotes real happiness and contentment." [69]

Socrates, Plato, and Aristotle recognized the principle of the "golden mean"; the Quakers and Transcendentalists in America such as Emerson and Thoreau were far more enchanted with developing an inner life than amassing material possessions.

Duane Elgin, author of *Voluntary Simplicity* writes that, *Simplicity is not an alternative lifestyle for a marginal few. It is a creative choice for the mainstream majority, particularly in developed nations.* We choose to simplify and live with a minimal footprint on the Earth, not in response to an environmentalist code, but because it fundamentally feels better and makes our lives more joyful.

Elgin shares eight "flowerings" in his "Garden of Simplicity":

1. *Uncluttered Simplicity*: Simplicity means taking charge of lives that are too busy, too stressed, and too fragmented. Simplicity means cutting back on clutter, complications, and trivial distractions, both material and nonmaterial, and focusing on the essentials— whatever those may be for each of our unique lives. As Thoreau said, "Our life is frittered away by detail…. Simplify, simplify." Or, as Plato wrote, "In order to seek one's own direction, one must simplify the mechanics of ordinary, everyday life."

2. *Ecological Simplicity:* Simplicity means choosing ways of living that touch the Earth more lightly and that reduce our ecological impact on the web of life. This life-path remembers our deep roots with the soil, air, and water. It encourages us to connect with nature, the seasons, and the cosmos. An ecological simplicity feels a deep reverence for the community of life on Earth and accepts that the nonhuman realms of plants and animals have their dignity and rights as well.

3. *Family Simplicity:* Simplicity means placing the well-being of one's family ahead of materialism and the acquisition of things. This expression of green living puts an emphasis on providing children with healthy role models living balanced lives that are not distorted by consumerism. Family simplicity affirms that what matters most in life is often invisible—the quality and integrity of our relationships with one another. Family simplicity is also intergenerational—it looks ahead and seeks to live with restraint so as to leave a healthy Earth for future generations.

4. *Compassionate Simplicity:* Simplicity means feeling such a strong sense of kinship with others that, as Gandhi said, we "choose to live simply so that others may simply live." A compassionate simplicity means feeling a bond with the community of life and being drawn toward a path of cooperation and fairness that seeks a future of mutually assured development for all.

5. *Soulful Simplicity:* Simplicity means approaching life as a meditation and cultivating our experience of direct connection with all that exists. By living simply, we can more easily awaken to the living universe that surrounds and sustains us, moment by moment. Soulful simplicity is more concerned with consciously tasting life in its unadorned richness than with a particular standard or manner of material living. In cultivating a soulful connection with life, we tend to look beyond surface appearances

and bring our interior aliveness into relationships of all kinds.

6. *Business Simplicity:* Simplicity means that a new kind of economy is growing in the world, with healthy and sustainable products and services of all kinds (home-building materials, energy systems, food production, transportation). As the need for a sustainable infrastructure in developing nations is being combined with the need to retrofit and redesign the homes, cities, workplaces, and transportation systems of developed nations, it is generating an enormous wave of green business innovation and employment.

7. *Civic Simplicity:* Simplicity means that living more lightly and sustainably on the Earth requires changes in every area of public life—from public transportation and education to the design of our cities and workplaces. The politics of simplicity is also a media politics, as the mass media are the primary vehicle for reinforcing—or transforming—the mass consciousness of consumerism. To realize the magnitude of changes required in such a brief time will require new approaches to governing ourselves at every scale.

8. *Frugal Simplicity:* Simplicity means that, by cutting back on spending that is not truly serving our lives, and by practicing skillful management of our personal finances, we can achieve greater financial independence. Frugality and careful financial management bring increased financial freedom and the opportunity to more consciously choose our

path through life. Living with less also decreases the impact of our consumption upon the Earth and frees resources for others. [70]

The Joy of Stillness

Industrial civilization is anything but still. From the moment we awake each day until we fall into our beds at night, our lives are usually frenzied and frantic with activity, tasks we must perform, goals we must achieve. Everything in our culture mitigates against slowing down, taking time, and being present. No wonder that the practice of mindfulness, now even becoming popular in corporate boardrooms, and other meditation practices are ubiquitous. No wonder that a book such as Eckhart Tolle's *The Power of Now* quickly sold millions of copies and instantly became a *New York Times* best seller.

Eckhart Tolle himself, who is succeeding in making *stillness* a household word, encapsulates in one paragraph the essence of joy in relation to stillness:

> Things and conditions can give you pleasure, but they cannot give you joy. Nothing can give you joy. Joy is uncaused and arises from within as the joy of Being. It is an essential part of the inner state of peace, the state that has been called the peace of God. It is your natural state, not something that you need to work hard for or struggle to attain. [71]

In the tradition of the great spiritual teachers such as Buddha, Ramana Maharishi, Krishnamurti, and the Dalai Lama, Eckhart's teaching focuses primarily on accessing and practicing the stillness that is inherent in consciousness. In *The Power of Now*, he writes:

> Paying attention to outer silence creates inner silence; the mind becomes still. A portal is opening up. Every sound is born out of silence, dies back into silence, and during its life span is surrounded by silence. Silence enables the sound to be. It is an intrinsic but unmanifested part of every sound, every musical note, every song, every word. This is why it has been said that nothing in this world is so like God as silence. [72]

We believe that there is absolutely no possibility of experiencing authentic joy unless one cultivates a daily practice of stillness. The madness of modernity demands this of us, and if we long to experience and radiate joy, we must immerse ourselves regularly and frequently in stillness. And as Eckhart reminds us, both outer and inner stillness are necessary, but even in the midst of the external cacophony of our frenetic milieu, with practice, we can access inner stillness.

The Joy of Authenticity

Modern, non-indigenous cultures are starving for authentic connection. We are lead to believe that social media and online dating websites will provide it for us, but we are relationship-illiterate. The proliferation of such organizations such as Marshall Rosenberg's Non-Violent Communication and a plethora of online Meetup groups are evidence of our hunger for authentic communication.

Yet in a happiness-obsessed culture, individuals have little tolerance for full-spectrum authenticity. In that milieu, it is acceptable to be authentic up to a certain threshold, beyond which people prefer only happy endings. Social critic James Howard Kunstler noted in his blog in 2002: "Life is tragic because of our consciousness that it comes to an end for us as individuals." [73] In other venues and podcasts, Kunstler often elaborates on the "tragic sense of life," meaning that every life has a beginning, a middle, and an end. So do nations or families or jobs or projects. Yet citizens of infantilized, inauthentic cultures prefer to believe that progress moves in only one direction: irrevocably forward. Wiser and more seasoned cultures have learned that as the saying goes, all good things come to an end. Accepting this is the crux of authenticity and deep wisdom. Moreover, if a tragic sense of life is absent, then we are likely to feel entitled to a pain-free existence where we need not be inconvenienced with unpleasant thoughts or conversations that include suffering.

Our ancient and indigenous ancestors knew that there is joy in experiencing authentic connection even if it includes suffering. The ancient Greek tragedians envisioned tragedy as catharsis. Its intention was not to make people sad but to infuse them with the truth of reality and the amazing range of human emotion. Why else do audiences feel joyful after a performance of King Lear—one of the most depressing plays in history? Because the play is authentic, and in it, the audience is not being lied to.

The Joy of Ritual

The word *ritual* literally means "to fit together." Humans create rituals in order to alleviate their sense of separation and affirm their connection with the Earth, with one another, and with the sacred. Ritual sacralizes time and space. Ritual time is not ordinary time; it is special and sacred. Ritual space is not ordinary space but rather space that is made sacred for a particular purpose.

Carl Jung believed that humans need a symbolic life. In our banal, literal, linear, industrialized world, ritual provides one of the few places where we can utilize and celebrate symbolism. "Only the symbolic life," Jung said, "can express the needs of the soul." [74]

When we create rituals, we are consciously bringing the sacred into our lives. Celebrating birthdays, anniversaries, graduations, weddings, births, and of course creating funeral or memorial rituals mark momentous transitions in our lives and affirm that the sacred inhabits all of our days and activities. As noted above in terms of the African grief ritual, not all rituals feel joyful in the moment, but they often infuse meaning, purpose, and authentic connection in the midst of loss or simply the seeming ordinariness of life.

Dagara shaman, Malidoma Somé, author of, *Of Water and the Spirit: Ritual, Magic and Initiation in the Life of an African Shaman,* writes, "Ritual facilitates and provides us with a unique channel to access higher power. Certain issues don't want to be resolved mechanistically. We don't have to know how the power works; we just have to show up and let the higher forces deal with the issues. The trap we feel inside ourselves is removed once we enter into sacred space. The energies know how to push obstacles out." [75]

As emphasized by Malidoma, it is less important to "know how it works" than to participate in the ritual and experience its healing results. When we employ ritual in the healing process, the end result is no longer entirely up to us. In fact, in ritual we surrender the outcome and allow ritual to "fit together" what is broken in the situation so that forces wiser and more expansive than the human ego and rational mind can assist us.

The Joy of Celebration and Abandonment to Ecstasy

Deeply embedded in ancient and indigenous cultures were regular celebrations, often based on seasons or annual occurrences such as harvests, as well as celebrations created for momentous occasions. Regardless of challenges or losses experienced by the community, celebrations were inherent in everyone's life.

In twenty-first century modernity, an occasion such as the first day of spring or the first day of winter is barely noticed, whereas in traditional cultures, the end of one season and the beginning of another was highly significant and required not merely observation but celebration and festivity.

In *Ecstasy: Understanding the Psychology of Joy,* Robert Johnson reminds us of the myth of Dionysius and the Dionysian experience in which "...we will recognize a long-forgotten part of ourselves that makes us truly alive and connects us with every living thing." [76] On the one hand, Dionysian ecstasy can result in either sacred celebration or profane madness, and in fact, a culture imprisoned by the rational mind that prizes composure and control is both terrified and titillated by ecstatic celebration.

Because our corporate culture does not value the world of the senses—"the world of poets, artists, and dreamers who show us the life of the spirit as seen through the senses," [77] we inhabit most of our days in the mind and resort to the emotional excess of rock concerts, extreme sports, cacophonous, violent movies, or mind-altering substances to satisfy our natural, human longing for ecstasy. One reason we love rock concerts is that they reproduce the permission that tribal societies experienced to shed the confines of ego identity and enter nakedly into the joy that creates reality. And as Robert Johnson concludes, "The loss of spiritual ecstasy in Western society has left a void that we fill in the only way we know how: with danger and excitement." [78]

Every year a spectacular festival, Burning Man, occurs in the Nevada desert and in 2015 drew a crowd of more than 70,000. According to Wikipedia, "At Burning Man the community explores various forms of artistic self-expression, created in celebration for the pleasure of all participants. Participation is a key precept for the community— selfless giving of one's unique talents for the enjoyment of all is encouraged and actively reinforced. Some of these generous outpourings of creativity can include experimental and interactive sculpture, building, performance, and art cars among other mediums, often inspired by the yearly theme, chosen by organizers. The event takes its name from its culmination, the symbolic, ritual burning of a large wooden effigy ("the Man") that traditionally occurs on the Saturday evening of the event." [79] Burning Man is an annual event which celebrates both the amazing creativity of human beings as well as the inevitability of destruction—a tribute to both new life and the impermanence of all things.

Author Chris Saade notes that we need to celebrate our defeats as well as our triumphs. "We need to bring honor and respect to our soul's worthy defeats," writes Saade. "The effort invested in their aftermath needs to be acknowledged and celebrated. Defeats are stepping-stones to amazing manifestations that bless many. These 'let us honor our defeats' parties will recognize and bless the spiritual audacity, the courageous quest, the visionary stretch forward, the fortitude of spirit expanded in times of reversal of fortune. These events will also affirm the gallantry of the work done. These 'heroic defeat parties' will also remind everyone that the trough of the wave is an intrinsic part of the wave and a necessary preparation for the sought-after crest. Ultimately, what we celebrate from a spiritual perspective is the heroic journey itself, with all its breakdowns and breakthroughs, defeats and memorable manifestations. We must remind each other that defeats encountered in the pursuit of love's aspirations are diamond-like memories of the soul. We must protect each other from the corrosive despair that can arise when setbacks happen. We are the ones who can uphold the great dignity and the value of our spiritual—and temporary—defeats." [80]

Whether our celebrations are ordinary and subdued in the terms of which Chris Saade speaks or noisy and dramatic in the context of a loud ritual or the drama and festivity of Burning Man, we must honor the flame of celebration and abandonment to ecstasy which aches to erupt from the soul and body, blazing forth in unequivocal testimony to our aliveness and passion.

Nowhere in modern literature is there a more exquisite call to our raw aliveness than the extraordinary poem by the inimitable, Jewel Mathieson in "We Have Come to Be Danced":

> We have come to be danced not the pretty dance not the pretty pretty, pick me, pick me dance but the claw our way back into the belly of the sacred, sensual animal dance the unhinged, unplugged, cat is out of its box dance the holding the precious moment in the palms of our hands and feet dance

> We have come to be danced not the jiffy booby, shake your booty for him dance but the wring the sadness from our skin dance the blow the chip off our shoulder dance the slap the apology from our posture dance

> We have come to be danced not the monkey see, monkey do dance one, two dance like you one two three, dance like me dance but the grave robber, tomb stalker tearing scabs & scars open dance the rub the rhythm raw against our souls dance

> WE have come to be danced not the nice invisible, self conscious shuffle but the

matted hair flying, voodoo mama shaman
shakin' ancient bones dance the strip us
from our casings, return our wings sharpen
our claws & tongues dance the shed dead
cells and slip into the luminous skin of love
dance

We have come to be danced not the hold
our breath and wallow in the shallow end
of the floor dance but the meeting of the
trinity: the body, breath & beat dance the
shout hallelujah from the top of our thighs
dance the mother may I? yes you may take
10 giant leaps dance the Olly Olly Oxen
Free Free Free dance the everyone can come
to our heaven dance

We have come to be danced where the
kingdom's collide in the cathedral of flesh
to burn back into the light to unravel, to
play, to fly, to pray to root in skin sanctuary
We have come to be danced WE HAVE
COME [81]

Welcoming the exuberance of Dionysius, celebrating
the "collision of kingdoms"—the sacred and the profane in
the "cathedral of flesh," let us be danced in divine ecstasy.

The Joy of Creating Sacred Space

In indigenous cultures, the village is often a sacred
mandala, and in ancient cultures, cities were frequently

constructed as sacred mandalas as well. Individual houses were temples to life. In the bland, linear design of modernity, we must ask how our personal lives and communities might function more vibrantly if our homes and neighborhoods were fashioned as sanctuaries of the sacred?

Jill Angelo writes in *Sacred Space: Turning Your Home into a Sanctuary* that "no matter what place each of us calls home, the very word strikes a chord deep inside each of us. Home means sanctuary, the place we can rest, relax, enjoy time with friends, learn, grow...and just be. Our homes say a lot about who we are and what we think is important in life." She offers "Ten Ways to Invite Transformation and Spring Energy into Your Home," and emphasizes that creating sacred spaces in our homes can be done very inexpensively. What is required is not financial investment but imagination and a heartfelt sense of what enhances our sense of the divine in our homes. Jill invites us to cultivate an attitude of reverence for our lives which extends to our living space.

1. When we learn to say "no" more often, it sets boundaries and clears repetitive patterns, allowing new energy to come in. For example: filling our calendars with too many appointments or events, not to disappoint the hosts.
2. We release psychic weight by letting go of physical weight: clothes that don't fit or furniture we no longer use.
3. Bring Mother Nature inside: grow an indoor herb garden; put fresh flowers in every room; hang a sprig of eucalyptus in the shower.

4. When we add a splash of our favorite color into our home and wardrobe, it brings immediate joy and happiness. Feel the energy shift.

5. We honor ourselves by repeating this phrase each day: "I am Sacred" because we are. We can feel our moods and spirits shift ever so slightly each time we offer this grace to ourselves.

6. We can heal the clutter and pain in our hearts by journaling and forgiving ourselves and those we know need to be forgiven.

7. Fuel our bodies—our temples—with the freshest local, organic foods we can. Let's say *no* to GMOs.

8. Declare "electronic free" moments, hours, or— better yet—days. In solitude, we hear the deeply nourishing silence that our soul craves.

9. While showering, we can recapture our awareness and energy by releasing anger, anxiety, stress and worry. As we lather and rinse, envision it all flowing down the drain.

10. By surrounding our Sacred Space with items that touch our hearts and essence, we tell visitors the story of our home. [82]

We can make our home into a temple in a thousand ways using color, texture, strategic placement of items, fragrances, music, fountains and more to create a nurturing, safe, and sacred sanctuary. In this way, we incessantly remind ourselves that our authentic home is not the unconsecrated functionality of corporate culture's soul-less residency, but rather a holy of holies for the heart.

The Joy of Creativity

Carl Jung frequently spoke of the *daimon* within the psyche, by which he meant the inner spirit or divine presence that can guide us—a guardian angel or a natural voice. This *daimon*, or as it was called in Latin, our *genius*, contains not only the Divine presence, but our gifts, talents, and proclivities as well. Jung frequently pointed to the similarity between the words *daimon* and *demon*. Simply put, he suggested that if we do not appreciate the daimon, it could become for us a demon.

In *Fate and Destiny: The Two Agreements of the Soul*, Michael Meade reminds us that "If the spirit companion within us is rejected or ignored for too long it can change from a beneficial daimon to an inner demon. The angel on one's shoulder can become a 'little devil' that gets a person into the wrong trouble. Many an inner demon was once a guiding spirit that was bottled up too long. Many a genius has turned against its host as a result of the ego-self persistently turning away from the genuine orientation of the soul…When it comes to issues of the divine, there can be no neutral condition; either we serve the 'higher purpose' seeded within us or else foster a distortion that can become demonic." [83]

Yet in a culture that does not recognize our daimon nor support our discovering and refining it, how do *we* nurture it? In indigenous cultures, the elders often recognize from the moment that a child is conceived that she or he is bearing specific gifts for the community which must be consciously tended and protected from birth, into and beyond the child's rite of passage and throughout adulthood. Tragically, in the milieu of industrial civilization, a child is born without a community of elders, and beyond parents, teachers, and possibly a written aptitude test, one typically discovers one's gifts on their own and is fortunate if the adults around them support them in cultivating those gifts.

We believe that all genius is creative and that the genius or daimon is inherently generative and only becomes destructive or "demonic" if ignored or distorted. Moreover, we have experienced that we are most authentically creative when we are most intimately connected with the sacred genius within. As Michael Meade explains:

> Becoming one's true self means revealing one's innate genius...The native genius residing within us bears the innate gifts and talents we bring to the world and it intends to give them...The primary agreement our souls have made before birth is to deliver our unique gifts to the world. [84]

Not every one of us is destined to become a Mozart or an Emily Dickinson, but each of us carries a particular "genius" which has nothing to do with how we might score on an intelligence test. To be human is to create, and anyone can write poetry, paint, sing, play music, or express their creativity in myriad ways. Nor is it necessary to be wealthy in order to create. Some of the most creative human beings survive in the deprivation of third-world villages or as homeless on the streets of first-world cities. Like Socrates who learned to play an instrument while waiting to be executed, people in prisons often become brilliant writers or accomplished artists. For example, Chicano activist and poet Luis Rodriguez learned to write in prison as a teenager; today he is an award-winning poet.

However, creativity must be viewed from a much broader perspective than the arts. Millions of individuals are currently discovering their daimon through gardening, permaculture design, and engagement in the healing arts. Expressing our creativity is simply allowing life to flow through us and touch the lives of all living beings, for as Michael Meade reminds us, "Our essential task in life is to awaken to the way that the eternal would speak through us...." [85]

What could possibly engender more joy?

The Joy of Community

It is important to notice the difference between "hanging out" or just being with other people and community. In this culture we often hear the expression "intentional community," but in fact, all authentic community is intentional because within the word "community" is the word "commune." When we commune with others, we share our time, energy, resources, or just simply our hearts for a specific purpose. We can commune with neighbors by getting to know them and thereby increasing the likelihood of mutual support in times of need. When we share neighborhood or community celebrations or rituals, we are communing, and as we work with residents of our local community to protect our region from degradation, crime, or disaster, we are experiencing and expressing the joy of community.

In recent years, farmers' markets and community gardens have brought local residents together in a manner not experienced for centuries in some regions. Within the past two decades a "revolution of local" has begun in many of the world's industrialized regions where people are discovering a new sense of camaraderie and pride in the community not felt for generations. More frequently grocery stores are advertising "locally grown" foods and other products as consumers increasingly prefer to buy items produced close to home.

In some aboriginal cultures of Australia, people love to sit on rocks naked and commune with each other in silence. While most members of Western culture have little patience with silence and are far too repressed to sit naked with neighbors, many individuals are discovering the joy of sitting together with friends and even strangers at sidewalk cafés or picnics, working together on community projects, and engaging in conversation with neighbors or even complete strangers.

The Joy of Solitude and Rest

Just as we crave the joy of communing with other human beings, we inherently need solitude. Amid the manic madness of industrial civilization, we often disconnect from our need for solitude and inwardly fear that if we slow down and unplug from both technology and people, we will become slothful, unproductive, or even lazy. In fact, a clamorous culture can become addictive, and being alone or estranged from distraction intolerable. In a 2014 study at Virginia and Harvard Universities, students "preferred a jolt of pain to being made to sit and think." According to the study, "To see if the effect was found only in students, the scientists recruited more than 100 people, aged 18–77, from a church and a farmers' market. They too disliked being left to their thoughts." [86] Does this not speak volumes about why so many individuals in our culture crave extreme sports, violent movies, and other forms of exaggerated stimulation in order to feel alive and not alone?

Solitude is different from stillness, which we noted above as absolutely necessary for our spiritual development and holistic well-being. Solitude may or may not feel joyful and may involve all sorts of emotions, but removing oneself from the horde with its demands and distractions is as necessary and salutary as stillness. All great spiritual teachers exemplify the need for withdrawing from their public leadership to a place of quiet, conscious aloneness.

Ideally, solitude is not about just being alone so that we can complete a project, but rather it is restorative and provides an opportunity to slow down and recharge. In solitude we have the opportunity to be present with our thoughts and emotions, to gain perspective, and to contemplate what actions we need to take going forward.

Related to solitude is simply the joy of resting—the joy of consciously giving oneself the time to relax without any purpose. Animals are superb teachers regarding the joy of resting because they shamelessly love resting, which keeps them in a state of equilibrium and well-being.

The Joy of Dreaming

In a highly extroverted culture it is rare to encounter individuals who are committed to consciously working with their dreams. The scientific revolution essentially declared that only waking consciousness, replete with linear thoughts, is of any value, and that dreams simply result from meaningless firings of synapses in the brain. Yet many individuals have discovered the power and practicality of working with their dreams.

One of the most important aspects of working with dreams is writing them down upon waking. Keeping a dream journal beside the bed and writing the dream as soon as possible after having it may be the beginning of a deeper and more intimate relationship with one's unconscious mind. Likewise, the more we write our dreams in a journal, the more we are communicating to the unconscious that we are listening to it, and therefore, the more information we are likely to receive. As this relationship between us and the unconscious becomes more vivid, we experience a subtle and amazing joy at the depth and wisdom of the guidance that the unconscious is always pouring forth. Over time, and with commitment to humble attention, we become increasingly integrated in soul and body, guided by the wisdom of our dreams. This integration opens us to peace, truth, and joy at deeper levels.

Most importantly, each person's dream is unique and should be interpreted from their perspective, not from a book of dream interpretation or another person's notion of what someone else's dream means. Equally important is remembering that each part of the dream represents a part of the psyche, and in most cases, dream objects and events are symbolic, not literal. For most non-indigenous members of Western culture, dreams are usually not prophetic but speak to the condition of the inner world as if presenting us with an X-ray of the psyche. It may be helpful to read the works of Carl Jung or Joseph Campbell to assist with discerning one's own dreams. It may also be helpful to tell a dream to a trusted friend, not for the purpose of receiving that person's interpretation, but because there is power in simply telling the story of the dream. In many indigenous cultures such as the Achuar tribe of the Amazon, members of the tribe meet very early in the morning with the shaman to discuss their dreams the night before, and the direction of the day is set by this discussion.

The Joy of Being With and Loving Animals

In "Song of Myself," Walt Whitman wrote:

> I think I could turn and live with animals, they are so placid and self-contain'd, I stand and look at them long and long. They do not sweat and whine about their condition, They do not lie awake in the dark and weep for their sins, They do not make me sick discussing their duty to God, Not one is dissatisfied, not one is demented with the mania of owning things, Not one kneels to another, nor to his kind that lived thousands of years ago, Not one is respectable or unhappy over the whole earth. [87]

Anyone who has a pet or beloved outdoor animal friend has experienced the joy of communing with them—watching them and delighting in their humor and play. Moreover, one cannot have a relationship with an animal without receiving their unconditional love. Thus animals are increasingly being included in settings that provide services to humans. Cats and small dogs are being included in nursing homes and assisted living residences as ambassadors of love and companionship. Because many people who enter human hospice programs have had to say goodbye to pets, pets are being employed in those programs. Hospice pet therapy has been found to help reduce physical pain, lower blood pressure, improve heart rates, provide a sense of overall comfort to the hospice patient, reduce feelings of loneliness and depression, and lower levels of anxiety. [88]

Some of the most dramatic studies of the effects of animals in institutional settings have been conducted in prisons. Research conducted by Alvernia University indicates that incorporating dog training programs in prisons tends to reduce depression and hostility among inmates, improve human relationships between inmates, and in many instances, reduce recidivism rates. Increasingly, research points to the power of the unconditional love of an animal to transform the psychology and behavior of prison inmates. [89]

One remarkable instance of the healing power of animals is the story of Tia Maria Torres, founder of the Villalobos Rescue Center in New Orleans, Louisiana. Tia created a pit bull rescue facility in Southern California, then moved the facility to New Orleans in 2011. What makes this rescue center unique is her commitment to hire only parolees to care for the dogs and assist her in rescuing them, then adopting the dogs to forever homes. Tia has stated on many occasions that rescuing dogs and hiring parolees to care for them is a way of giving both the animals and humans a second chance. She also notes that when she moved her facility to New Orleans, she became a resident of "the city of second chances." Her *Animal Planet* reality show "Pit Bulls and Parolees" is now in its eighth season and opens with her personal core belief: "My mission is to rescue, and my hope is that one day, I won't have to." "Pit Bulls and Parolees" is an epic saga not only of second chances for abused and neglected dogs, but also for parolees whose lives have been transformed by their constant care of animals and the compassionate mentoring of Tia. [90]

Endless Flames of Joy

A flatline culture does not understand joy and therefore, cannot offer anything but an endless quest for happiness and momentary eruptions of shallow self-indulgence. This chapter has offered a number of flames of joy that potentially mitigate the damage visited upon us by the adversaries of joy and have the capacity to reconnect us with the source of all joy—divine ecstasy, divine love, divine beauty. No one understood this more than Rumi, who wrote: *Straddle the horse of joy. It is here the moment of our reunion. The drum of the coming true of promises is beating. The pathway of heaven is being swept. Your joy is now.* [91]

SUGGESTED PRACTICES

**What is your emotional reaction to the flames of joy outlined in this chapter?

**Choose one flame that especially resonates for you and write about it for a few minutes in your journal or elsewhere.

**Choose one flame that you feel may be lacking in your current life experience. How might you encourage and increase this flame of joy?

**Take time to write or journal about the relationship between joy and sorrow in your life. Has sorrow at times deepened your joy? Have you sometimes felt joy in the midst of sorrow?

**Contemplate deeply Jewel Mathieson's poem "We Have Come to Be Danced." We suggest not only thinking and possibly writing your responses in a journal, but actually moving your body in response to the emotions that the poem evokes in you. *Feel* in your body the sense of *being danced.*

CHAPTER 5

Dialogue on the Road to Joy

In this book we have offered our perspective on joy as the ultimate nature of reality quite simply because both of our long individual journeys have proven to us that it is. We did not arrive at this conclusion as a result of a lifetime of privilege or some random ability to avoid suffering. In fact, who we are today has been dictated *by* suffering and our response to it. Throughout our lives, adversity has been "unpredictably consistent" in the sense that we have been unable to escape it, and in fact, have come to a point in the journey in which we no longer seek to avoid suffering at all cost, for we have discovered that the *actual* cost of doing so is the loss of the gold that lies in the shadow and in our living from the perspective of "tragic optimism," as Victor Frankl has named it.

Thus, we have chosen in this final chapter of the book to share with you, dear reader, some of the key aspects of our journeys that have made the writing of this book both possible and compelling for both of us. Our hope is that our sharing will inspire and support you in settling for nothing less in your own pilgrimage than the radical joy we have articulated in the pages above.

Thus we have chosen to engage in the dialogue below and share it with you:

**Tell me five things right now that give you joy.

Carolyn: My dog, the work I do, living in the foothills of the Rockies, friendships with allies, music and art all give me profound joy.

Andrew: The music of Bach, my cat Jade lying in my arms in the morning, teaching Christian mysticism on the internet, walking around Paris, sacred relationships of all kinds.

**Describe the three most important experiences that taught you that joy is the essential nature of reality.

Andrew: In 2001 I had meditated for three days without food by the sea in South India in a place in which I've been initiated many times into mystical reality—Mahabalipuram. As dawn broke over the sea, I saw the whole of the scene in front of me become more and more transparent, like a very delicate Chinese painting on glass. A white light, brilliant and tender, seeped into and through everything. I walked on the beach in a state of calm bliss and looked up as the sun, which seemed now to be moving within me, soared free of a cluster of clouds, and threw a ball of light across the sea to my feet. This miraculous experience convinced me of the truth of what I had been studying for weeks of the Saivite mystics—that the whole universe is a dance of blissful light energy and that awakening is awakening to being one of the dancing cells in the great Dancer's cosmic body. There are no words to describe the effortless, spacious, serene, healing, utterly free ecstasy that springs from the heart of such a realization. And throughout the years that have followed, whatever has happened in my life, this experience has glowed for me as a sign of ultimate truth.

The second experience I'd like to share is one with the Dalai Lama. I've had the honor of knowing him for thirty years and am intensely devoted to him. In 2006 in a dream, I found myself kneeling at his feet, looking up into his radiant face in a small temple. He put his hands on my head, and my whole being filled with a soft crystalline, sensuous rapture in which every single cell was dancing. I heard him say, "This is the bliss of those who give everything away. This is the bliss of those who know that we are here to serve all beings until that time when all beings are liberated. This is the bliss of the bodhisattva. Live in this bliss and give everything away, and you will be free." I woke astounded and understood beyond thought that the Buddha of Compassion had revealed to me that not only was joy the essential nature of reality, but that a human being could live in that joy if, like the joy that creates everything, he or she constantly pours himself or herself out for no reason and with no agenda except that of compassion. Although in the years that followed I cannot say I have lived constantly in this joy, I know it to be seeded in the core of my being, and when I need it, through the extraordinary grace of His Holiness, it bubbles up within me.

The third experience is one of total heartbreak giving birth to unimaginable revelation. Perhaps the greatest love of my life was my cat, Topaz, who loved me with a passion and hilarity and wild energy and total abandon that I had never experienced from any other being. I thought that we would live for a long time together, but I was only graced with five years with him. Returning from a trip to New York to the log cabin in Arkansas in which I was living, I found him dramatically emaciated. I took him immediately to the veterinarian who told me that he was riddled with cancer and begged me calmly to spare him any more pain by euthanizing him then and there. The brutality of this experience was like being hacked to my knees by an axe. I returned home with his body in a cardboard box and put a Buddha head on the box. The next day my landlord dug a hole under a tree, and I went to collect the box for the burial. It is very difficult to express what happened next. I opened the box, saw a shriveled body of what had been my cat, and started to laugh wildly. I knew beyond thought or reason in that moment that all I was seeing was an old husk that Topaz had leapt free of. I knew he was not dead. I knew he was eternally alive in the golden light which had sent him to me in the first place. And I knew that the love we had experienced, because it was so whole and complete, could never die. The biggest suffering of my life birthed the most healing revelation. Since this experience, I have known at a far deeper level than before that all true love and all true acts of service are in their nature timeless and have consequences far beyond anything that reason can understand. This has given me a steady, joyful courage to continue doing my work in what is an obviously darkening world.

Carolyn: Throughout my adult life, as a result of growing up in an extremely dysfunctional, fundamentalist Christian family, I did not experience joy as I know it today. At an early age, in Sunday school, I learned about having "joy, joy, joy down in my heart, down in my heart, down in my heart to stay," but I realize today that what I experienced as joy as a child was not the joy of which we speak in this book.

In my teenage years, one of the few places where I could experience joy was in my relationship with my horses. Riding and caring for them brought great joy even as in the course of about three years, two of them died and one became lame. Nevertheless, the thrill and freedom of riding remained, and in my fifties while living in the Southwest, I returned to riding on a number of occasions. Nothing could compare with the joy I experienced sitting on a horse with whom I had developed a trusting relationship, feeling its power and strength on the one hand, and its willingness to obey my commands and plod faithfully along the trail on the other. The joy of riding my horses while living in an oppressive, fundamentalist Christian household was a preview of future instances throughout my life of my inherent wild, instinctual nature riding roughshod over caution and dogma to the wind.

In the sixties, the wild woman in me was compelled to experiment with psychedelics as were so many of my generation. While I began a meditation practice that I have continued to this day, that was also a time of experiencing profound ecstasy through LSD. The cynical, atheistic intellectual that I had become was inexplicably humbled by the cellular, bone marrow impact of an expansion of consciousness for which there were neither words nor precedent. Whereas I had come to believe that no reality existed beyond the five physical senses, I was dumbfounded by the altered states of awareness produced by my psychedelic adventures. At the culmination of one LSD exploit, I found myself sitting in a tulip garden very early on a spring morning feeling in every cell of my body that the tulips and I were of the same flesh and that there was absolutely no separation between us. I would never view the world or my life the same after those moments of intimacy with nature.

On yet another occasion, and without the use of psychedelics, I experienced a similar union with nature in a place called McGurk Meadow in Yosemite National Park in 1994. In total isolation and far from civilization, I wandered for at least an hour feeling, touching, smelling, tasting, and listening to every aspect of nature within view. As I allowed myself to fully engage with every sight, sound, and texture, I was deluged with the unprecedented, and again cellular, realization that I was one with every blade of grass, every pine needle, every birdsong, every bubbling utterance from a mountain stream, every rock, every stone. Without the use of chemicals to alter my awareness, these sensations of unity pulsed through my body, causing me to burst into tears repeatedly in an eruption of divine ecstasy. In those moments, the "every" became the One.

If I may beg the reader's forgiveness for sharing a fourth experience from current time, I'd like to share that shortly after my ecstatic encounters in McGurk Meadow, I learned to tell stories using an African drum as accompaniment. For more than two decades, storytelling with the drum has filled me with unmitigated joy as the words and the drumbeats pulsate through and from my body. Even more thrilling than my own experiences of joy in drumming and storytelling are the reports of listeners who tell me that something in their bodies or psyches shifted dramatically.

AFTERWORD

"I would love to kiss you"
"The price of kissing is your life"
Now my loving is running toward my life
shouting, "What a bargain! Let's take it!"
~Rumi~

The attainment of wholeness requires
one to stake one's whole being.
Nothing less will do; there can be no easier
conditions, no substitutes, no compromises. [92]
~Carl Jung~

Throughout this book we have noted numerous individuals who have fashioned lives of radical joy, and often, suffering was a fundamental aspect of their journey. To reiterate what we stated earlier, the pursuit of happiness asks nothing from us, but returning to joy in a flatline culture demands everything—or as Rumi states, "The price of kissing is your life."

Like Victor Frankl, Nelly Toll's life was profoundly altered by the holocaust as a child living in Poland when forced into hiding from the Nazis during World War II. She dared to dream, imagining a better world that manifested in her creation of nearly 60 lovely watercolor paintings. Today at 81, Nelly Toll is enjoying a harvest of reward as her paintings are on exhibition around the world. From a very early age, Nelly discovered the power of the flames of creativity and art to infuse her with joy even in moments of fear and despair. At the opening of her exhibit in Berlin, she stated, "I hope that generations to come will look at this and know that atrocities made me do this." [93]

In the Hindu tradition, joy is often referred to as "bliss." The beloved Krishnamurti wrote that, "Happiness and pleasure you can buy in any market at a price. But bliss you cannot buy for yourself or for another. Happiness and pleasure are time-binding. Only in total freedom does bliss exist. Pleasure, like happiness, you can seek, and find, in many ways. But they come, and go. Bliss that strange sense of joy has no motive. You cannot possibly seek it. Once it is there, depending on the quality of your mind, it remains timeless, causeless, and a thing that is not measurable by time." [94]

American social critic and activist Barbara Ehrenreich states that, "…if happiness is contentment, why settle for that? What about adventure, exhilaration, or creative obsession? In our focus on the nebulous goal of 'happiness,' we seem to have forgotten the far more acute and searing possibility of joy." [95]

Only in total freedom does bliss exist, Krishnamurti reminds us. In order to experience the quality of joy to which this book invites you to return, it is necessary to cease pursuing the husks of happiness with which corporate culture tantalizes us and settle for nothing less than "the searing possibility of joy."

In order to reclaim joy as the ultimate nature of reality and the fundamental birthright of our humanity, a price must be paid, and that price is nothing less than the total renunciation of the heart-numbing, soul-murdering vapidity of a flatline existence as we embrace the heart-throbbing, love-laden passion of unimaginable joy in action and realize the vision given to Andrew Harvey which began this book.

Many centuries after Rumi, Rainer Maria Rilke grasped the ferocity of the price to be paid for our return to joy as well as the ecstasy awaiting our commitment to total aliveness, so beautifully articulated in *As Once the Winged Energy of Delight*:

> Wonders happen if we can succeed in passing through the harshest danger; but only in a bright and purely granted achievement can we realize the wonder... Take your practiced powers and stretch them out until they span the chasm between two contradictions...For the god wants to know himself in you [96]

ENDNOTES

1. Rainer Maria Rilke, *Letters on Life*, edited and translated by Ulrich Baer, Modern Library, 2006, p. 175
2. *The Essential Mystics*, edited with introduction by Andrew Harvey, Harper One, 1997, pp. 36–37
3. Robert Johnson, *Ecstasy: Understanding the Psychology of Joy*, Harper, 1987, p. 12.
4. "Barbara Ehrenreich: The Relentless Promotion of Positive Thinking Has Undermined America," Alternet, October 9, 2009, http://www.alternet.org/story/143187/barbara_ehrenreich%3A_the_relentless_promotion_of_positive_thinking_has_undermined_america
5. Office of Tibet website: http://tibetoffice.org/tibet-info/invasion-after
6. Lyrics of "Something Beautiful Remains," song lyrics: http://www.lyricsfreak.com/t/tina+turner/something+beautiful+remains_20137732.html
7. *I Am Malala: The Girl Who Stood Up for Education and Was Shot by the Taliban*, Back Bay Books, 2015, p. 300
8. [*Laudato Si* http://w2.vatican.va/content/francesco/en/encyclicals/documents/papa-francesco_20150524_enciclica-laudato-si.html]

9. Homily of Pope Francis, March 24, 2013, St. Peter's Square, http://w2.vatican.va/content/francesco/en/homilies/2013/documents/papa-francesco_20130324_palme.html

10. Being Catholic, John Paul II http://www.catholiccincinnati.org/59916/we-need-saints/

11. Website of White Lion Trust, http://whitelions.org/about/meet-linda-tucker/

12. Linda Tucker, More To Life Magazine Interview, http://www.moretolifemag.co.uk/2016/09/saving-white-lions/

13. Andrew Harvey & Seymour Bernstein, *Play Life More Beautifully*, 2016, Hay House, p. 189

14. Mark Nepo, Beliefnet Interview, http://www.beliefnet.com/columnists/awakeintheworld/2013/07/1661.html#ixzz40oxfa200

15. Joseph Campbell, *The Power of Myth*, Anchor Publishing, 1991, p. 84

16. Francis Weller, *The Wild Edge of Sorrow*, North Atlantic Books, 2015, p. 103

17. Ibid, 104–105

18. Philip Shepherd, *New Self, New World: Recovering Our Senses in the Twenty-First Century*, North Atlantic Books, 2016, p. 37–38

19. [Thich Nhat Hahn, "Buddhist Views on Oneness and Humanity, Peace and the Environment," http://www.geni.org/globalenergy/research/geni-initiative-and-world-religions/what-unites-us-is-stronger-than-our-differences/Publication-buddhism.pdf

20. Shepherd, *New Self, New World*, p. 50

21. Ibid, p. 48

22. Ibid, p. 50

23. "The Corporate Media State Has Deformed American Culture—Time to Fight Back," Chris Hedges, Alternet, June 29, 2009, http://www.alternet.org /story/140997/the_corporate_media_state_has_def ormed_american_culture_--_time_to_fight_back

24. *Democracy Now* interview with Jane Mayer, January 20, 2016, http://www.democracynow.org/2016/1/20/ dark_money_jane_mayer_on_how

25. Ibid.

26. "How The Koch Brothers Have Changed America," Interview with Jane Mayer, *Rolling Stone,* February 14, 2016, http://www.rollingstone.com/politics/news/ author-jane-mayer-on-how-the-koch-brothers-have-changed-america-20160214

27. John Taylor Gatto, *Dumbing Us Down: The Hidden Curriculum of Compulsory Schooling,* New Society Publishers, 2002, p. 14

28. Rainer Maria Rilke, *Letters on Life*, edited and translated by Ulrich Baer, Modern Library Paperback, 2006, pp. 111–112

29. "Sunday Morning," by Wallace Stevens, http://www. bartleby.com/265/355.html

30. Kakuzo Okakura, *The Book of Tea,* available online at everything2.com

31. "The Top Ten Reasons Why Science Is Another Religion," by Cortical Rider, December, 2012, http://listverse.com/2012/12/15/top-10-reasons-science-is-another-religion/

32. "Religion and Science," *New York Times,* Albert Einstein, November 9, 1930.

33. Robert Johnson, *Ecstasy*, p.11

34. *New Self, New World*, pp. 19-20

35. Andrew Harvey, *Radical Passion: Sacred Love And Wisdom In Action*, North Atlantic Books, 2012, p. xv

36. Robert Johnson, *Ecstasy*, pp. 48–49

37. Ibid, p.12

38. "Creation as the Body of God," by Richard Rohr, *Spiritual Ecology: The Cry of the Earth*, edited by Llewellyn Vaughan-Lee, Golden Sufi Center, 2014, p. 238

39. Ibid, p.241

40. Charles Upton, *Day and Night on the Sufi Path*, Sophia Perennis, 2015, pp.32–33

41. Ibid, p. 421

42. Rainer Maria Rilke, *Letters on Life*, Modern Library Paperback, 2006, p. 23

43. Victor Frankl, *Man's Search for Meaning,* Beacon Press, 2000, p. 162.

44. Andrew Harvey, *The Essential Mystics*, p, 135

45. Mahatma Gandhi, *Selected Political Writings*, Hackett Publishing, 1966, p. 47

46. Cited in *The Hope: A Guide To Sacred Activism*, by Andrew Harvey, Hay House, p. 185.

47. Philip Shepherd, *New Self, New World*, p. 275

48. Ibid, p. 277

49. Richard Rohr, *Falling Upward: A Spirituality for the Two Halves of Life*, Josey-Bass, 2011, p. 117

50. Jung, Memories, Dreams, & Reflections, pp. 451–452 http://www.amazon.com/Memories-Dreams-Reflections-Richard-Winston/dp/B0038KC6BK/ref=pd_sim_sbs_14_3?ie=UTF8&dpID=41q58

Y4y5gL&dpSrc=sims&preST= AC UL160 SR120 %2C160 &refRID=0D8DB09DGAE6FN1CCB6F

51. Andrew Harvey, *Light Upon Light*, Jeremy Tarcher, 1996, p. 3

52. "Living One's Oneness," Lewellyn Vaughan-Lee, Huffington Post, April 30, 2012, http://www. huffingtonpost.com/llewellyn-vaughanlee/mysticism-living-loves-oneness b 1304518.html

53. Cynthia Bourgeault, *The Wisdom Jesus: Transforming Heart and Mind—A New Perspective on Christ and His Message*, Shambala, 2008, pp. 78-79

54. Andrew Harvey, *Light Upon Light*, p. 96

55. Drew Dellinger, *Love Letter to the Milky Way*, White Cloud Press, 2011, p. 66

56. Thomas Berry, *The Sacred Universe: Earth, Spirituality, and Religion in the Twenty-First Century*, Columbia University Press, 2009, p. 92

57. Mary Oliver, *Thirst: Poems by Mary Oliver*, Beacon Press, 2006, p. 1 [poem fragment]

58. "UN Environment Programme: 200 Species Extinct Every Day, Unlike Anything Since Dinosaurs Disappeared 65 Million Years Ago," Huffington Post, August, 2010, http://www.huffingtonpost.com/2010/08/17/un-environment-programme- n 684562.html

59. David Abrams, *Becoming Animal: An Earthly Cosmology*, Pantheon, 2010, p. 3

60. Ibid, p. 80

61. "The Joy of Being" DVD, Denmark retreat, 2012

62. Joseph Campbell, *The Inner Reaches of Outer Space: Metaphor as Myth and as Religion*, New World Library, 2002, p. 128

63. "Ten Ways to Invite Transformation and Spring Energy into Your Home," Jill Angelo, Elephant Journal, February, 2014, http://www.elephantjournal.com/2014/02/10-ways-to-invite-transformation-spring-energy-into-your-home-jill-angelo/

64. Naomi Shihab Nye, *Words Under The Words: Selected Poems, The Eighth Mountain Press*, 1994 [poem fragment]

65. *The Archdruid Report,* "The Burden of Denial," John Michael Greer, April, 2015, http://thearchdruidreport.blogspot.com/2015/04/the-burden-of-denial.html

66. Eckhart Tolle, *The Power of Now*, New World Library, 1999, p. 197

67. Francis Weller, *The Wild Edge of Sorrow*, pp. xxii-xxiii

68. Mary Oliver, *Evidence*, Beacon Press, 2009, p. 13

69. M.K. Gandhi, *Hind Swaraj or Indian Home Rule*, Ahmedabad, Navajivan, 1938, p. 90

70. "Voluntary Simplicity," by Duane Elgin, The Daily Good, October 22, 2013, http://www.dailygood.org/story/559/voluntary-simplicity-duane-elgin/

71. Eckhart Tolle, *The Power of Now*, p. 187

72. Ibid, p. 136

73. "Clusterfuck Nation Chronicles," November, 2002, http://www.kunstler.com/mags_diary5.html

74. "The Symbolic Life," published in the *Collected Works*, Vol. 18, pp. 625–628. Transcript from shorthand notes from a seminar talk given on April 5, 1939, to the Guild of Pastoral Psychology, London. Jung approved the transcript

75. Menstuff Website interview, 2005, Reid Baer, http://www.menstuff.org/columns/overboard/some.html

76. Robert Johnson, E*cstasy*, p. 3

77. Ibid, p. 12

78. Ibid, p. 17

79. Burning Man: https://en.wikipedia.org/wiki/ Burning_Man

80. Chris Saade, *Second Wave Spirituality: Passion for Peace, Passion for Justice*, North Atlantic Books, Berkeley, CA, 2014 pp. 173–174

81. Published with permission of Jewel Mathieson

82. Jill Angelo, *Sacred Space: Turning Your Home into a Sanctuary*, Tayenlane, 2016, pp. 33-35

83. Michael Meade, *Fate and Destiny: The Two Agreements of the Soul*, Greenfire Press, 2012, p. 148

84. Ibid, p. 6

85. Ibid, p. 7

86. ["Shocking but true: students prefer jolt of pain to being made to sit and think," The Guardian, July 3, 2014, https://www.theguardian.com/science/2014/jul/03/ electric-shock-preferable-to-thinking-says-study

87. "Song Of Myself," Walt Whitman, https://www. poetryfoundation.org/poems-and-poets/poems/ detail/45477

88. Crossroads Hospice, https://crhcf.org/Blog/ what-is-hospice-pet-therapy/

89. Alvernia University, http://online.alvernia.edu/ how-dog-training-is-affecting-prison-rehabilitation/

90. Wikipedia: Pit Bulls And Parolees, https://en.wikipedia. org/wiki/Pit_Bulls_%26_Parolees

91. Andrew Harvey, *Light Upon Light*, p.52

92. Carl Jung, *Psychology and Religion*, Second Edition, Princeton University Press, 1969, p. 556

93. "Exhibit of Jewish Artists' Holocaust Works Opens in Berlin," Business Insider, January, 2016, http://www.businessinsider.com/ap-exhibit-of-jewish-artists-holocaust-works-opens-in-berlin-2016-1

94. J. Krishnamurti, *Meditations*, 1969, Part 10

95. Barbara Ehrenreich, "Happy Now?" John Hopkins Magazine, September 3, 2010, http://archive.magazine.jhu.edu/2010/09/happy-now/

96. *The Selected Poetry of Rainer Maria Rilke*, edited by Stephen Mitchell, Vintage, 1989, p. 261

ABOUT THE AUTHORS

Andrew Harvey

Andrew Harvey is Founder Director of the Institute of Sacred Activism, an international organization focused on inviting concerned people to take up the challenge of our contemporary global crises by becoming inspired, effective, and practical agents of institutional and systemic change, in order to create peace and sustainability. Sacred Activism is a transforming force of compassion-in-action that is born of a fusion of deep spiritual knowledge, courage, love, and passion, with wise radical action in the world. The large-scale practice of Sacred Activism can become an essential force for preserving and healing the planet and its inhabitants. His work can be explored in depth at www.andrewharvey.net

Carolyn   Baker is the author of *Love In The Age Of Ecological Apocalypse: The Relationships We Need To Thrive* (2015) as well as *Collapsing C o n s c i o u s l y : T r a n s f o r m a t i v e Truths For Turbulent Times* (2013). Her previous books are and *Navigating The Coming Chaos: A Handbook For Inner Transition* (2011) and *Sacred Demise: Walking The Spiritual Path Of Industrial Civilization's Collapse* (2009). With Guy McPherson, Carolyn co-authored *Extinction Dialogs: How To Live With Death In Mind* (2014) and published *Dark Gold: The Human Shadow And The Global Crisis* (2016). She lives and writes in Boulder, Colorado and manages her website www.carolynbaker.net. A former psychotherapist and professor of psychology and history, Carolyn is a life coach and consultant for people who want to live more resiliently in the present as they prepare for the future. Her podcast, the New Lifeboat Hour airs weekly online.